# INNOVATIONS AND FUTURE DIRECTIONS IN THE **BEHAVIOURAL** AND **COGNITIVE** **THERAPIES**

edited by
Ross G. Menzies, Michael Kyrios, Nikolaos Kazantzis

**AUSTRALIAN**ACADEMIC**PRESS**

First published 2016 by:
Australian Academic Press Group Pty. Ltd.
18 Victor Russell Drive
Samford Valley QLD 4520, Australia
www.australianacademicpress.com.au

National Library of Australia Cataloguing-in-Publication entry :

Title: Innovations and future directions in the behavioural and
cognitive therapies / Ross G. Menzies,
Michael Kyrios, Nikolaos Kazantzis,
editors.

ISBN            9781922117700 (paperback)
ISBN            9781922117717 (ebook)

Subjects: Cognitive therapy--Forecasting.
Behavior therapy--Forecasting.

Other Creators/Contributors:
Menzies, Ross G., editor.
Kyrios, Michael, editor.
Kazantzis, Nikolaos, editor.

Dewey Number: 616.891425

Publisher: Stephen May
Copy Editor: Rhonda McPherson
Cover design: Tim Everton
Cover image: Shutterstock
Page design & typesetting: Australian Academic Press
Printing: Lightning Source

# Contents

## Anxiety and Its Disorders

## Obsessive Compulsive and Related Disorders

## Trauma, PTSD and Grief

## Obesity and Eating Disorders

## Depression and Bipolar Disorders

## Psychosis

## Alcohol and Substance Misuse

## Health and Chronic Medical Disorders

## E-therapy

## Training, Practice and Access Issues

Dedication

For my great loves, Margot, Rachel, Henry, Matilda and little Jude – RGM
For Georgia, Mietta, James and my parents - MK
For Sophia – NK

x

# Preface

The concept for a comprehensive volume on innovations and future directions in the behavioural and cognitive therapies arose from early discussions within the Australian team bidding to host the *World Congress of Behavioural and Cognitive Therapies* (WCBCT). It seemed a shame that so many wonderful presentations from past events were simply lost after the event. Much of the data presented would inevitably find its way into a large number of disparate scientific journals, but an account of the state of knowledge about cognitive-behaviour therapy (CBT) and the treatment of the mental disorders at the time of each congress has not been documented until now.

In this volume, we have provided a book of readily consumable essays from leading figures across all areas relevant to CBT. The chapters were commissioned only months before the 8th WCBCT and the volume therefore gives us a clear sense of 'the state of play' at the beginning of 2016. In addition, the contributors were explicitly encouraged to make their chapters 'opinion pieces'. The authors were not required to present research findings, but were asked to give a summary of their work and the broader field. In addition, they were required to provide explicit sections on the clinical implications of their work and the directions for future research and practice.

Having conceived the book, how did we go about selecting the contributors? In many ways, this was the toughest job of all. The WCBCT brings the 'best of the best' from across mental health together at one place and time. With over 1000 presentations on offer, how could we choose the material for the volume? Fortunately, the scientific committee had developed a rigorous system of review for all submissions that we decided to use for our selection. Each paper and symposium was judged by a minimum of two independent reviewers. They were scored on a range of criteria including scientific quality, relevance of the topic to the WCBCT audience, level of innovation, and likely impact on the field. To ensure that the chapters were sufficiently broad in their coverage, we considered only the symposium submissions in the final selection. The 63 submissions that scored above 19 out of 25 on the independent reviews were offered inclusion in the volume. An impressive 53 took up our offer, and their chapters make up the final book.

The theme of the 8th WCBCT was Advances and Innovations in the Behavioural and Cognitive Therapies across the World. It was a particularly inclusive event, calling for papers in a broad range of subthemes or topic areas. The book is divided into sections that mirror these subthemes. We were fortunate to receive high quality symposium submissions in the majority of the listed topics, and so the breadth of our volume is impressive. The list of contributors is also impressive — a veritable 'who's who' of clinical psychology and related fields. Over 190 leading authors from across Britain, Europe, North and South America, Asia and Australia have contributed to this volume.

We hope you will enjoy this collection of short chapters. It is our view that they will bring you quickly up to date with the world of CBT in 2016.

**Ross G. Menzies, Michael Kyrios, and Nikolaos Kazantzis**

# About the Editors

**Ross G. Menzies**

A/Professor Menzies completed his undergraduate, masters and doctoral degrees in psychology at the University of NSW. He is currently an Associate Professor in Health Sciences at the University of Sydney. In 1991, he was appointed founding Director of the Anxiety Disorders Clinic at the University of Sydney, a post which he held for over 20 years. He is the past NSW President, and twice National President, of the Australian Association for Cognitive Behaviour Therapy (AACBT). He is the editor of Australia's national CBT journal, Behaviour Change, and has trained psychologists, psychiatrists and allied health workers in CBT around the globe. A/Professor Menzies is an active researcher with two decades of continuous funding from national competitive sources. He has produced 7 books and more than 150 journal papers and book chapters. Most recently, he was the President and Convenor of the 8th World Congress of Behavioural and Cognitive Therapies.

**Michael Kyrios**

Professor Mike Kyrios is Director of the Research School of Psychology at the Australian National University and President of the Australian Psychological Society (APS). He also holds honorary positions at the University of Melbourne and Swinburne University. Mike was elected a Fellow of the APS in 2007, received the 2013 Ian M. Campbell Memorial Prize in

Clinical Psychology and was awarded a Citation for Excellence from the American Psychological Association in 2011. Mike was Scientific Chair for the 2010 International Congress of Applied Psychology and 2016 World Congress of Behavioural and Cognitive Therapies. He currently sits or has been on the editorial Boards of, amongst others, Behavior Therapy, Behavioural and Cognitive Psychotherapy and the International Journal of Psychology. Mike has received over $17 million in grant funding and has over 150 scholarly publications. He has been a frequent invited workshop and master clinician presenter, keynote speaker and consultant to government.

### Nikolaos Kazantzis

Nikolaos Kazantzis, PhD is Program Director for clinical psychology and Associate Professor at the Institute for Cognitive and Clinical Neurosciences (MICCN) at Monash University. He also serves as Director of MICCN's Cognitive Behaviour Therapy Research Unit. A/Prof Kazantzis received post-doctoral training in the early 2000s at the Beck Institute under the direct teaching of Aaron T. Beck, MD., and Judith S. Beck, PhD. Among many awards, he is recipient of the 'Beck Scholar Award' from Aaron T. Beck for excellence in contributions to CBT. He has over 100 scholarly publications, including the forthcoming book 'The Therapeutic Relationship in Cognitive Behavior Therapy.' He has developed training programs for over 6,000 professionals, and has presented workshops in 20 countries. A/Prof Kazantzis is Associate Editor for 'British Journal of Clinical Psychology', 'Cognitive Therapy and Research,' 'International Journal of Cognitive Therapy', Deputy Scientific Chair for the 8th WCBCT, and IACP Australian delegate and board member.

# List of Contributors

| | |
|---|---|
| Claire Ahern | Swinburne University of Technology, Melbourne, Australia |
| Ola Ahmed | University of New South Wales, Sydney, Australia |
| Nathan Alkemade | University of Melbourne, Melbourne, Australia |
| Stephanie Allen | Life & Mind Psychology, Sydney, Australia |
| Yvette Alway | Monash University, Melbourne, Australia |
| Tanya Arabatzoudis | Swinburne University of Technology, Melbourne, Australia |
| Henry Austin | University of Western Australia, Perth, Australia |
| Andrew Baillie | Macquarie University, Sydney, Australia |
| Amanda Baker | University of Newcastle, Newcastle, Australia |
| Ryan Balzan | Flinders University, Adelaide, Australia |
| Marthinus Bekker | Australian National University, Canberra, Australia |
| Michael Berk | Deakin University, Melbourne, Australia |
| Sunil Bhar | Swinburne University of Technology, Melbourne, Australia |
| Max Birchwood | University of Warwick, Coventry, UK |
| Jon Fauskanger Bjaastad | Stavanger University Hospital, Stavanger, Norway |
| Ingvar Bjelland | Haukeland University Hospital, Bergen, Norway |
| Mark Boschen | Griffith University, Southport, Australia |
| Caroline Braet | Ghent University, Ghent, Belgium |
| Richard Bryant | University of New South Wales, Sydney, Australia |
| Kay Bussey | Macquarie University, Sydney, Australia |
| Yulisha Byrow | Macquarie University, Sydney, Australia |
| Richard Cash | University of Melbourne, Melbourne, Australia |
| Weilynn C. Chang | Massachusetts General Hospital, Boston, USA |
| Marie Chellingsworth | University of East Anglia, Norwich, UK |
| Junwen Chen | Flinders University, Adelaide, Australia |

| | |
|---|---|
| Helen Christensen | University of New South Wales, Sydney, Australia |
| Katie Chung | University of New South Wales, Sydney, Australia |
| Jason M. Coates | University of Queensland, Brisbane, Australia |
| Wendell Cockshaw | Queensland University of Technology, Brisbane, Australia |
| James Collard | CBT Australia, Cairnmillar Institute, Melbourne, Australia |
| Jason P. Connor | University of Queensland, Brisbane, Australia |
| Jacqueline Costello | Centre for Mental Health, Australian Defence Force |
| Sarah Cox | Flinders University, Adelaide, Australia |
| Cathy Creswell | University of Reading, Reading, UK |
| Paul Cromarty | Flinders University, Adelaide, Australia |
| Erica Crome | Macquarie University, Sydney, Australia |
| Katie S. Dawson | University of New South Wales, Sydney, Australia |
| Peter J. de Jong | University of Groningen, Groningen, The Netherlands |
| Mark Deady | University of New South Wales, Sydney, Australia |
| Blake F. Dear | Macquarie University, Sydney, Australia |
| Thilo Deckersbach | Massachusetts General Hospital, Boston, USA |
| Keith S. Dobson | University of Calgary, Calgary, Canada |
| Helen F. Dodd | University of Reading, Reading, UK |
| Emma Doolan | University of New South Wales, Sydney, Australia |
| Darin D. Dougherty | Massachusetts General Hospital, Boston, USA |
| Marina Downing | Monash University, Melbourne, Australia |
| Sarah J. Egan | Curtin University, Perth, Australia |
| Lara J. Farrell | Griffith University, Gold Coast, Australia |
| Daniel B. Fassnacht | Australian National University, Canberra, Australia |
| Sally Fitzpatrick | Macquarie University, Sydney, Australia |
| Krister Westlye Fjermestad | University of Oslo, Oslo, Norway |
| Lorraine Fliek | Maastricht University, Maastricht, The Netherlands |
| Vincent J. Fogliati | Macquarie University, Sydney, Australia |
| David Forbes | University of Melbourne, Melbourne, Australia |
| Jonathan Foster | Curtin University, Perth, Australia |
| Kathryn Gilson | Monash University, Melbourne, Australia |
| Alexandra K. Gold | Massachusetts General Hospital, Boston, USA |
| Hermine Graham | University of Birmingham, Birmingham, UK |
| Rachel Graville | Curtin University, Perth, Australia |
| Matthew J. Gullo | University of Queensland, Brisbane, Australia |

| | |
|---|---|
| Andrew Gumley | University of Glasgow, Glasgow, Scotland |
| Anthony Gunn | University of Sydney, Sydney, Australia |
| Kim Haesen | University of Leuven, Leuven, Belgium |
| Kerrie Haines | Monash University, Melbourne, Australia |
| Natasha Hansen | University of Colorado, Boulder, USA |
| Bente S. M. Haugland | Uni Research Health, Bergen, Norway |
| Sarra Hayes | Curtin University, Perth, Australia |
| Nathan Haymes | Australian National University, Canberra, Australia |
| Casey M. Hearing | Massachusetts General Hospital, Boston, USA |
| Einar R. Heiervang | University of Oslo, Oslo, Norway |
| Megan Henderson | Chris Mackey & Associates, Geelong, Australia |
| David A. Heyne | Leiden University, Leiden, The Netherlands |
| Leanne Hides | Queensland University of Technology, Brisbane, Australia |
| Stefan Hofmann | Boston University, Boston, USA |
| Susan Hogan | Flinders University, Adelaide, Australia |
| Jennifer Hudson | Macquarie University, Sydney, Australia |
| Shin-ichi Ishikawa | Doshisha University, Kyoto, Japan |
| Lisa Iverach | University of Sydney, Sydney, Australia |
| Louise Johns | University of Oxford, Oxford, UK |
| Kristy Johnstone | Flinders University, Adelaide, Australia |
| Nienke C. Jonker | University of Groningen, Groningen, The Netherlands |
| Naomi Kakoschke | Flinders University, Adelaide, Australia |
| Yoshihiro Kanai | Tohoku Gakuin University, Sendai, Japan |
| Junichiro Kanazawa | Health Sciences University of Hokkaido, Hokkaido, Japan |
| Robert Kane | Curtin University, Perth, Australia |
| Nadine A. Kasparian | University of New South Wales, Sydney, Australia |
| David J. Kavanagh | Queensland University of Technology, Brisbane, Australia |
| Frances Kay-Lambkin | University of Newcastle, Newcastle, Australia |
| Nikolaos Kazantzis | Monash University, Melbourne, Australia |
| Peter J. Kelly | University of Wollongong, Wollongong, Australia |
| Eva Kemps | Flinders University, Adelaide, Australia |
| Lucy Kenny | University of New South Wales, Sydney, Australia |
| Daniel King | University of Adelaide, Adelaide, Australia |
| Naoko Kishita | University of East Anglia, Norwich, UK |
| Arne Kodal | University of Bergen, Bergen, Norway |

| | |
|---|---|
| Michael Kyrios | Australian National University, Canberra, Australia |
| Ken Laidlaw | University of East Anglia, Norwich, UK |
| Nicole K. Lee | Flinders University, Adelaide, Australia |
| Krystal Lewis | University of Virginia, Charlottesville, USA |
| Belinda Liddell | University of New South Wales, Sydney, Australia |
| Peter Lovibond | University of New South Wales, Sydney, Australia |
| Robyn Lowe | University of Sydney, Sydney, Australia |
| Fiona Maccallum | University of New South Wales, Sydney, Australia |
| Chris Mackey | Chris Mackey & Associates, Geelong, Australia |
| Colin MacLeod | University of Western Australia, Perth, Australia |
| Madhavan Mani | Queensland University of Technology, Brisbane, Australia |
| Ann Martin | University of New South Wales, Sydney, Australia |
| Brandy R. Maynard | Saint Louis University, St. Louis, USA |
| Peter M. McEvoy | Curtin University, Perth, Australia |
| Brittany C. McGill | University of New South Wales, Sydney, Australia |
| Tony McHugh | University of Melbourne, Melbourne, Australia |
| Adam McKay | Monash University, Melbourne, Australia |
| Anna McKinnon | Macquarie University, Sydney, Australia |
| Hamish J. McLeod | University of Glasgow, Glasgow, Scotland |
| Richard Meiser-Stedman | University of East Anglia, Norwich, UK |
| Rachel E. Menzies | University of Sydney, Sydney, Australia |
| Ross G. Menzies | University of Sydney, Sydney, Australia |
| Ann Meulders | University of Leuven, Leuven, Belgium |
| Daniel Michelson | University of Oxford, Oxford, UK |
| Katherine Mills | University of New South Wales, Sydney, Australia |
| Gerri Minshall | The Children's Hospital at Westmead, Sydney, Australia |
| Richard Moulding | Deakin University, Melbourne, Australia |
| Michelle L. Moulds | University of New South Wales, Sydney, Australia |
| Peter Muris | Maastricht University, Maastricht, The Netherlands |
| Frank Muscara | University of Melbourne, Melbourne, Australia |
| Akiko Nakagawa | Chiba University, Chiba, Japan |
| Yasmina Nasstasia | University of Newcastle, Newcastle, Australia |
| Maja Nedeljkovic | Swinburne University of Technology, Melbourne, Australia |
| Jill M. Newby | University of New South Wales, Sydney, Australia |
| Nicola C. Newton | University of New South Wales, Sydney, Australia |

| | |
|---|---|
| Angela Nickerson | University of New South Wales, Sydney, Australia |
| Andrew A. Nierenberg | Massachusetts General Hospital, Boston, USA |
| Reginald Nixon | Flinders University, Adelaide, Australia |
| Lies Notebaert | University of Western Australia, Perth, Australia |
| Sue O'Brian | University of Sydney, Sydney, Australia |
| Meaghan O'Donnell | University of Melbourne, Melbourne, Australia |
| Monica O'Kelly | Monash University, Melbourne, Australia |
| Tom Ollendick | University of Virginia, Charlottesville, USA |
| Mark Onslow | University of Sydney, Sydney, Australia |
| Jinnie Ooi | University of East Anglia, Norwich, UK |
| Fumiyo Oshima | Chiba University, Chiba, Japan |
| Lars-Göran Öst | Stockholm University, Stockholm, Sweden |
| Ann Packman | University of Sydney, Sydney, Australia |
| Rosanna Pajak | University of New South Wales, Sydney, Australia |
| Pandora Patterson | University of Sydney, Sydney, Australia |
| Kiri Patton | University of Queensland, Brisbane, Australia |
| Mia Pellizzer | Flinders University, Adelaide, Australia |
| Yael Perry | University of New South Wales, Sydney, Australia |
| Amy T. Peters | University of Illinois at Chicago, Chicago, USA |
| Lorna Peters | Macquarie University, Sydney, Australia |
| Jennie Ponsford | Monash University, Melbourne, Australia |
| Imogen C. Rehm | Swinburne University of Technology, Melbourne, Australia |
| David Rimmington | Flinders University, Adelaide, Australia |
| Joanne Ross | University of New South Wales, Sydney, Australia |
| Susan L. Rossell | Swinburne University of Technology, Melbourne, Australia |
| David Said | Centre for Mental Health, Australian Defence Force |
| Suraj Samtani | University of New South Wales, Sydney, Australia |
| Davina Sanders | Queensland University of Technology, Brisbane, Australia |
| Ursula Sansom-Daly | University of New South Wales, Sydney, Australia |
| Sophie C. Schneider | Macquarie University, Sydney Australia |
| Ghislaine Schyns | Maastricht University, Maastricht, The Netherlands |
| Irene Sclare | South London and Maudsley NHS Foundation Trust, London UK |
| Fiona Shand | University of New South Wales, Sydney, Australia |
| Reneta Slikboer | Swinburne University of Technology, Melbourne, Australia |

| | |
|---|---|
| Paul Stallard | University of Bath, Bath, UK |
| Jonathan P. Stange | Temple University, Philadelphia, USA |
| Lexine Stapinski | University of New South Wales, Sydney, Australia |
| Lauren G. Staples | Macquarie University, Sydney, Australia |
| Stoyan Stoyanov | Queensland University of Technology, Brisbane, Australia |
| Mirjana Subotic | Macquarie University, Sydney, Australia |
| Louisa G. Sylvia | Massachusetts General Hospital, Boston, USA |
| Alexander Tee | Flinders University, Adelaide, Australia |
| Maree Teesson | University of New South Wales, Sydney, Australia |
| Neil Thomas | Swinburne University of Technology, Melbourne, Australia |
| Nickolai Titov | Macquarie University, Sydney, Australia |
| Aki Tsuchiyagito | Osaka University, Osaka, Japan |
| Adrienne Turnell | Australian National University, Canberra, Australia |
| Cynthia M. Turner | University of Queensland, Brisbane, Australia |
| Kirsten Vale | Flinders University, Adelaide, Australia |
| Karolien van den Akker | Maastricht University, Maastricht, The Netherlands |
| Jens Van Lier | University of Leuven, Leuven, Belgium |
| Laura Vandeweghe | Ghent University, Ghent, Belgium |
| Leentje Vervoort | Ghent University, Ghent, Belgium |
| Pedro Vieira da Silva | Universidade Federal do Rio Grande do Sul, Porto Alegre, Magalhaes, Brazil |
| Tracey Wade | Flinders University, Adelaide, Australia |
| Polly Waite | University of Reading, Reading, UK |
| Claire E. Wakefield | University of New South Wales, Sydney, Australia |
| Jade Walters | Griffith University, Southport, Australia |
| Haley J. Webb | Griffith University, Gold Coast, Australia |
| Gro Janne H. Wergeland | Haukeland University Hospital, Bergen, Norway |
| Ross White | University of Glasgow, Glasgow, Scotland |
| Reinout Wiers | University of Amsterdam, Amsterdam, The Netherlands |
| Quincy Wong | Macquarie University, Sydney, Australia |
| Dana Wong | Monash University, Melbourne, Australia |
| Viviana M. Wuthrich | Macquarie University, Sydney, Australia |

Section 1


Child, Adolescent and Youth Mental Health

# The development of anxiety in childhood and adolescence: The transmission of cognitive biases

Jinnie Ooi, Helen F. Dodd, Lorraine Fliek, and Peter Muris

## Overview

Threat-related information processing biases such as interpretation bias (a tendency to disproportionately interpret ambiguous information as threatening) have been implicated in the onset and maintenance of anxiety disorders. However, the origins of these biases remain unclear. Tentative evidence suggests that cognitive biases can be learned, and there is some indication that these biases might be acquired from significant others, such as parents, peers, and romantic partners. This chapter will highlight existing work on the association and/or transmission of anxious cognitions within close relationships, including those relevant at a range of developmental stages (i.e., childhood, adolescence, early adulthood).

## Major Findings

Research exploring the transfer of cognitive biases has predominantly focused on the transmission from parents to their children. Initial evidence of this intergenerational transmission comes from studies showing a correlation between child and parent interpretation bias as well as research demonstrating that a child–parent discussion can affect children's anxiety-related responses. As such, it is assumed that parents play a role in the formation of children's cognitive biases. Recent findings support this proposition, indicating that parental verbal threat information transmission may induce anxiety in their children (aged 9–12 years) by influencing their cognitive biases.

This intergenerational transmission of anxious cognitions seems to occur at various developmental stages. To begin with, parents may influence children's cognitive bias in early childhood. More precisely, it has been demonstrated that the way parents tell their children stories (measured using written story-stems) is associated with preschool-aged children's interpretation bias. Further, in middle childhood, children's fear levels are influenced by parental verbal information. Research has demonstrated that parents given threatening information about novel animals transfer this information to their offspring, which installs higher levels of fear in the children when compared to the children of parents given positive information. In line with the above, recent research indicates that parental verbal feedback influences children's threat information search bias (a tendency to search for negative information); children who were encouraged by their parents to ask for more threatening information about novel animals showed an increase in threat information search bias and fear beliefs, while those who were directed by their parents towards asking for more positive information showed a decrease in threat information search bias and fear beliefs.

Importantly, parents who are more anxious instill more threatening cognitions in their children, indicating a possible pathway through which anxious parents might enhance children's risk for developing anxiety. For instance, when parents were not given explicit instructions regarding the verbal feedback to be given to their children, those with higher levels of trait anxiety more frequently transmitted their own threat information search bias to their children after working together on an information search task, thereby also increasing children's fear levels.

Interestingly, recent research has shown an association between parent and offspring biases even when the children are young adults. However, it is currently unclear whether the transmission of bias via parents occurred earlier in childhood and was then maintained until young adulthood, or whether parents continue to influence their children's biases even during later stages of development. Likewise, it remains unclear to what extent young adults and their parents might influence each other's biases reciprocally.

Besides the parent–child relationship, anxious cognitions may also be associated in other forms of close relationships. A recent study has demonstrated for the first time that close friends in middle childhood exhibit shared patterns of fear beliefs and avoidance behaviours of novel animals, and that these fear responses became even more similar following a joint discussion about fear-related issues. Furthermore, there are also indications that young adult romantic partners might influence each other's anxious cognitions. Although their biases did not become more similar after discussing ambiguous scenarios together, there was an overall decrease in interpretation bias following the interaction.

As a whole, recent research is beginning to shed light on how anxious cognitions might be acquired, suggesting that such cognitions may be transmitted not only within the parent–child relationship, but also in other forms of close relationships across various stages of development.

## Clinical Implications

The increasing evidence for the intergenerational transmission of anxious cognitions suggests that including parents in cognitive-behaviour therapy (CBT) with their children to modify parents' anxious cognitions could yield a better therapeutic outcome, compared to a standalone CBT for children. Given the above findings, the therapeutic benefit of including parents may well depend on the parents' own anxiety level and anxious cognitions. With regards to other forms of close relationships, the limited work in this area currently renders it difficult to draw definitive recommendations for clinical practice. Even though there is some evidence for an association and/or transmission within close friendships and romantic relationships, the effect sizes of these associations/effects are fairly modest. Therefore, instead of including close friends and romantic partners in CBT, it may be more beneficial for individuals undergoing treatment for anxiety to identify close friends or partners who may be influencing their cognitions and to be given strategies on how to discuss cognitions adaptively.

Furthermore, it is plausible that significant others could play an active role in modifying cognitions in anxious individuals. Parent-administered cognitive bias modification of interpretations (CBM-I) training through storytelling has been shown to be effective in reducing interpretation bias and social anxiety symptoms in school-aged children. This form of training could potentially be extended not only to younger children, but also to other forms of close relationships. For instance, school-based preventive efforts could teach pairs of close friends to discuss and resolve their worries positively.

Such interventions could be a cost-efficient strategy to facilitate early preventive gains for at-risk populations.

## Future Directions

As existing research indicates that anxious cognitions can be acquired within close relationships, future efforts should primarily be directed at exploring whether significant others can play a constructive role in modifying anxious cognitions. One way to do this would be to extend existing CBM-I work, making use of individuals who have a close relationship with at-risk or anxious individuals. Additionally, prospective studies and research in clinical populations are needed to advance work in this area.

## Further Readings

Muris, P., van Zwol, L., Huijding, J., & Mayer, B. (2010). Mom told me scary things about this animal: Parents installing fear beliefs in their children via the verbal information pathway. *Behaviour Research and Therapy*, 48(4), 341–346.

Remmerswaal, D., Muris, P., & Huijding, J. (2015). Transmission of cognitive bias and fear from parents to children: An experimental study. *Journal of Clinical Child & Adolescent Psychology*, 1–13.

Ooi, J., Dodd, H. F., & Walsh, J. (2015). Shared cognition in childhood anxiety: Interpretation bias in preschool children and their parents. *Journal of Child and Family Studies*, 24(11), 3413–3422.

## Chapter 2

# Low intensity and school-based interventions for children with anxiety: Outcomes, challenges and future directions.

Paul Stallard, Cathy Creswell, Krystal Lewis, Tom Ollendick and Polly Waite

### Overview

Anxiety disorders are one of the most common mental health problems experienced by children and adolescents. They have a significant impact upon all aspects of everyday functioning including family relationships, friendships, academic attainment and social life. Often childhood anxiety persists and increases the risk of anxiety, depression, substance misuse and educational underachievement in late adolescence and early adulthood.

Effective psychological interventions are available with those based on cognitive-behaviour therapy (CBT) having the largest evidence base. While this is encouraging, traditional interventions are very intensive, requiring 9–16 hours of face-to-face meetings. The availability of appropriately trained CBT therapists is limited. There are increasing demands for specialist child and adolescent mental health services while funding for services has become very challenging. Developing low intensity interventions would provide a way of using limited clinical expertise more efficiently.

In addition to improving accessibility to psychological services there is also a need to enhance emotional wellbeing through preventive interventions. Only one third of children with anxiety disorders are ever referred to specialist child and adolescent mental health services for treatment. This has led to interest in the development of preventative interventions in community settings such as schools where CBT-based programs can be widely provided. However little is known about whether these interventions are acceptable to schools and if they are sustainable.

## Major Findings

Recent studies have explored whether low intensity interventions such as bibliotherapy, with limited therapist time, can be effective. Lewis and Ollendick evaluated a four-week bibliotherapy program designed to treat young children with persistent and interfering nighttime fears. Nine children between 5 and 7 years of age with a specific phobia of dark/dark alone were randomised to one of three multiple baseline control conditions (1, 2, or 3 weeks). Parents read a self-help book to their children over four weeks while engaging in activities prescribed in the book. The book was based on CBT principles. The parents were seen for only one pre-bibliotherapy session at which time the book was given to them and they were instructed on how and when to read the book to their child and how to interact with them about any concerns raised while reading the book. Pre-post group analyses revealed that 8 of the 9 children demonstrated clinically significant change in phobia severity — a rate equalling that observed in clinic-based CBT programs. In addition, decreases in child-reported nighttime fears were observed, as were parent-reported decreases in separation anxiety and increases in the number of nights children slept in their own bed.

Similar positive findings of bibliotherapy were reported by Creswell who randomised 136 children (aged 5–12) to either guided parent-led CBT or solution-focused therapy. Both interventions were low intensity and involved 5 hours of contact (by phone or face-to-face) with a primary child and adolescent mental health worker. The two treatments did not differ on clinical outcomes (diagnostic status, global improvement and parent/child reported symptoms) with good outcomes achieved across both arms (e.g., 59%–69% very/much improved post-treatment). However, economic analyses revealed significant cost-benefits of guided parent-delivered CBT in comparison to solution-focused therapy due primarily to the reduced travel and administrative burden associated with this approach.

Low intensity interventions can also be provided online with structured CBT programs being well suited for adaptation and delivery via computer. Waite provided 60 adolescents with an anxiety disorder with a computerised CBT intervention BRAVE-Online. All adolescents received BRAVE-Online, either immediately or following a 12-week wait, with or without additional parent sessions. The program was effective in that 40% of adolescents were free of their primary anxiety disorder immediately post-treatment and this rose to 60% at 6-month follow-up. There was not a significant difference in treatment outcome between adolescents whose parents had or had not received sessions. This suggests that clinical services with limited clinical resources should not routinely commit additional resources to the provision of parent sessions.

In terms of prevention, Stallard found promising reductions in anxiety at 12 months from a CBT program (FRIENDS for Life) universally provided in schools to 9- to 10-year-old children (*n* = 1362). Interviews with 115 children found high levels of satisfaction with the program and examples of ongoing skills usage. Teachers (*n* = 47) had mixed views and were concerned about how the program fitted with the school curriculum and the additional time required for delivery. Almost half of the teachers were unable to identify any tangible changes in the children's behaviour. While prevention programs might be effective and acceptable to children they need to fit within busy school timetables and be perceived as helpful by teachers if they are to be sustainable.

## Clinical Implications

These findings suggest that low intensity interventions supported by books or computerised programs achieve comparable outcomes to longer, more clinician intensive interventions. The need for fewer clinic attendances and face-to-face meetings with a specialist therapist might be more convenient for patients and be an efficient and cost-effective way of delivering services. However, interventions need to be perceived as helpful and fit within existing structures and pathways if they are to be sustainable.

Clinical services should consider developing a stepped care approach to the prevention and treatment of anxiety disorders. The first step would be preventive interventions, coproduced with school staff, based on empirically supported models, but which fit within the practical timetabling constraints of schools. The second would be low-intensity interventions for those with emerging or established anxiety disorders. Low cost interventions offer increased choice and can be flexibly tailored to the needs and preferences of children and parents. The third step would be intensive interventions for those with complex, comorbid and enduring anxiety disorders.

## Future Directions

Further work is required to establish the benefits of low intensity interventions. In particular, studies need to determine their acceptability and to understand who they work for and who they do not. The optimal length of treatment needs to be determined and the longer-term effects and cost-benefits established. The use of technology including mobile phone apps to deliver and support interventions should be explored. Finally, the social acceptability of prevention and low intensity interventions needs to be established. If interventions are not perceived by schools, clinicians, children or families to be acceptable or do not readily fit within a community context or care pathway, they will not be sustainable.

## Further Readings

Bennett-Levy, J., & Farrand, P. (2010). Low intensity CBT models and conceptual underpinnings. In J. Bennett-Levy, D. A. Richards, & P Farrand, H. Christensen, K. M. Griffiths, D. J. Cavanaugh, B. Klein, M.A. Lau, J. Proudfoot, L. Writterband, J. White, & C. Williams (eds.). *Oxford guide to low intensity CBT interventions*. Oxford, England: Oxford University Press.

Creswell, C., Waite, P., & Cooper, P. J. (2014). Assessment and management of anxiety disorders in children and adolescents. *Archives of Disease in Childhood, 99*(7), 674–678.

Skryabina E., Morris J., Byrne D., Harkin N., Rook S., & Stallard, P. (in press). Child, teacher and parent perceptions of the FRIENDS classroom-based universal anxiety prevention programme: A qualitative study. *School Mental Health*.

Chapter 3

# Long-term outcome and predictors of outcome in CBT for youth anxiety

Jon Fauskanger Bjaastad, Gro Janne Henningsen Wergeland, Krister Westlye Fjermestad, Arne Kodal, Bente Storm Mowatt Haugland, Ingvar Bjelland, Einar R. Heiervang, Lars-Göran Öst, and Jennie L. Hudson

## Overview

Several meta-analyses and reviews have found that cognitive-behaviour therapy (CBT) is an efficacious treatment for anxiety disorders in children and adolescents (hereafter youths). The vast majority of studies are conducted within university-based anxiety research clinics (efficacy trials), and recent studies in community clinics (effectiveness trials) indicate that CBT is also effective in these settings. Although CBT is regarded as efficacious, the current evidence base suggests that up to 40% of youths receiving CBT do not obtain diagnostic recovery or significant symptom reduction. Furthermore, few studies have investigated outcome beyond one-year post-treatment, thus more research is needed to establish the durability of CBT effects. Research investigating potential predictors of both short- and long-term outcome is needed to inform continuous improvement of CBT programs for anxiety disorders in youth. This chapter will provide the reader with an overview of current research findings of long-term outcome and predictors of outcome in CBT for youth anxiety.

## Major Findings

The majority of CBT trials for youth anxiety including follow-up assessments have examined outcome up to one-year post-treatment. A handful of studies have applied longer follow-up periods, including 2 years, 3 years, 5 years, 6 years, 7.4 years and 16.2 years follow-up. Results from these long-term studies generally suggest treatment gains are maintained or improved for a considerable amount of treatment responders. The longest follow-up study to date, with a mean follow-up of 16.2 (range = 6.7–19.2) years after treatment, suggests that youths who did not respond successfully to CBT more often had panic disorder, drug abuse, alcohol dependence and suicidal ideation in adulthood compared to responders. Reviews of outcome predictors in CBT for youth anxiety disorders have found some evidence that child factors (i.e., baseline symptom severity, comorbidity, principal diagnosis of social anxiety disorder and level of impairment) and parent factors (i.e., internalizing psychopathology) are associated with poorer outcomes. These findings are, however, inconsistent across studies. In the largest predictor study to date, predictors of treatment response across 11 sites in Australia, Denmark, Norway, Switzerland, United Kingdom, United States, and the Netherlands were examined, including 1519 children (5–18 years) receiving CBT for their principal anxiety disorder. Results suggested that a principal anxiety diagnosis of social anxiety disorder, non-anxiety comorbidity (both mood and externalising disorders), and parental psychopathology were associated with poorer treatment outcomes after CBT. In sum, some predictors are identified, but findings are inconsistent across studies and more research into predictors is warranted.

## Clinical Implications

CBT is an efficacious treatment for youth anxiety disorders and results from long-term studies show promise for durability of treatment gains. Since treatment response may depend on principal anxiety disorder, parental psychopathology, pre-treatment symptom severity, level of impairment, and comorbidity, these are, so far, the primary factors to consider for clinicians in treatment planning. Youth with social anxiety disorder may benefit from a specific intervention (e.g., Social Effectiveness Therapy for Children and Adolescents [SET-C]) rather than a generic intervention (e.g., Coping Cat, Cool Kids, FRIENDS). CBT for anxiety disorders in youth have traditionally consisted of generic programs where exposure is targeted towards the principal anxiety disorder. There may be a need for a more specific treatment intervention focusing on models specific for social anxiety disorder, which is the case with CBT for social anxiety disorder in adults. Clinicians should also be aware that parental psychopathology is associated with poorer treatment outcome. Helping parents seek treatment if needed, and/or taking the parental psychopathology into consideration during treatment (e.g., how can we help these parents with the prescribed exposure work, how does their behaviour affect and maintain the youth's symptoms and how to assist them in developing more helpful parenting behaviour?), may be indicated. As higher pre-treatment symptom severity and impairment is negatively associated with treatment outcome, clinicians may consider adjusting the 'dose' of CBT, although the effect of this has yet to be empirically tested. Such adjustments could involve planning additional and more frequent sessions compared to standard CBT treatment, using more intensive treatment formats (e.g., sessions with a duration of half or whole days, conducted daily over the course of a week which allows for more focused exposure work) and/or consider combining CBT with sertraline, which has been found to produce a superior response rate. Finally, given that comorbid externalizing and mood disorders are associated with poorer outcome, modular-based CBT targeting mood and externalizing disorders in addition to anxiety disorders may be beneficial, although more research is needed to evaluate this.

## Future Directions

There is a need for more research on long-term effects of CBT for youth anxiety disorders and predictors of long-term outcome. More effectiveness studies should be conducted to evaluate the efficacy of CBT for youth anxiety disorders in regular outpatient settings, and more research on the implementation of CBT is needed. Further research on characteristics of non-responders may give indications for how CBT for anxiety disorders in youth may be improved. Future studies should investigate whether CBT interventions with differing doses of therapist contact (e.g., more therapist contact, more frequent sessions, and longer sessions) improves outcomes for youths with higher baseline-symptom severity and higher levels of impairment. Finally, the evaluation of stepped-care programs will be important to inform effective service delivery and how to best utilise treatment resources (e.g., who benefits from low-intensity CBT vs high-intensity CBT).

## Further Readings

Knight, A., McLellan, L., Jones, M., & Hudson, J. (2014). Pre-treatment predictors of outcome in childhood anxiety disorders: a systematic review. *Psychopathology Review, 1,* 77–129.

Benjamin, C.L., Harrison, J.P., Settipani, C.A., Brodman, D.M., & Kendall, P.C. (2013). Anxiety and related outcomes in young adults 7 to 19 years after receiving treatment for child anxiety. *Journal of Consulting and Clinical Psychology, 81*(5), 865–876.

Wergeland, G.J., Fjermestad, K.W., Marin, C.E., Bjelland, I., Haugland, B.S.M., Silverman, W.K., ... Heiervang, E.R. (2016). Predictors of treatment outcome in an effectiveness trial of cognitive behavioral therapy for children with anxiety disorders. *Behaviour Research and Therapy, 76,* 1–12.

Chapter 4

# Exploring research across different countries, languages and formats, of the FRIENDS programs

Marthinus Bekker

## Overview

Child and family focused cognitive-behaviour therapy (CBT) have progressed substantially and are considered the treatment of choice for most childhood internalizing disorders. Mental health difficulties among young people are abundant in our society with many estimating that 20% of young people worldwide are experiencing mental health difficulties. What makes this an even bigger challenge is that only 20% of young people experiencing mental health difficulties are accessing appropriate treatment. Time-limited CBT-based treatments make good sense to address this discrepancy. However, many barriers remain that continue to hinder access to treatment. Governments and health boards are struggling to meet demand often only seeing the most severe cases. Contributing to this is the cost of delivering treatments, with many treatments being delivered individually, adding up to a significant cost to public health organisations or individuals seeking private services. Much of the literature to date focuses on developing more effective treatments with significant success but it could be argued that research and practice need to focus on delivering CBT-based interventions wider, earlier, and in more accessible ways. A group of researchers is taking on these challenges and they are using the FRIENDS programs, a suite of evidence-based, developmentally targeted intervention and prevention programs, across the world in many languages and continents.

## Major Findings

Research and practice have often been focused on developed western nations and more populated areas within these nations, and they are often still bound to clinics and hospitals. These factors can limit the ability for them to reach their intended populations. For CBT-based interventions to increase their transportability they need to be trialled and adapted for developing nations, low socioeconomic areas, rural and remote areas, and closer to young people in settings like schools.

Several FRIENDS researchers are exploring delivery in schools and one group in particular have been implementimng FRIENDS in low socioeconomic schools in Mexico, showing reductions in anxiety and other psychosocial difficulties ($p < .01$) at post-intervention as well as an increase in proactive coping strategies ($p < .05$). Demonstrating the use of CBT-based programs in more challenging settings that break down many barriers to engagement.

With many mental health services straining under the increasing demand often only the most severe cases are seen. These are young people who have come across circumstances that have interacted with their vulnerabilities and have not had the skills to cope with these challenges. By providing

CBT-based skills as ways of being more resilient before diagnoses apply, we can give them a strong fence round the top of the cliff rather than the ambulance down the valley. The economic benefits of providing preventative interventions have been clearly shown and the benefit to the individual and their family of preventing mental illness is obvious.

A large-scale preventative trial in the United Kingdom (UK) recently demonstrated, that a school-based delivery of the FRIENDS program could be effective in reducing ratings on a measure of child anxiety and depression. At 12 months there was a reduction of child-reported scores of anxiety and depression in the health led FRIENDS program as compared to usual school provision ($p = .043$). This effect persisted at 24 months although the difference between it and usual school provision was not apparent anymore, meaning that levels of anxiety and depression reduced in both groups, but much faster in the intervention group. These results are in line with a large meta-analytic review that showed overall effect sizes of $d = 0.18$ in preventative programs, with FRIENDS programs producing substantially higher results with effects of $d = 0.30$.

CBT-based intervention although already time limited are still most commonly delivered in individual or family sessions over a period of three or more months. This brings up several limiting factors to their efficiency, such as the resources required to provide clinicians and the organisation of families to attend three or more months of sessions. Offering interventions in groups and delivering interventions in shorter time frames, all provide more accessible interventions that reduce barriers to engagement.

Delivery of the FRIENDS program in a Norwegian Community Clinic recently demonstrated that group delivered FRIENDS was as effective as individually delivered

FRIENDS, with no difference between delivery methods. Results showed that 35% of participants no longer met diagnostic criteria for a primary anxiety disorder post-treatment in both individual and group formats which increased to over 46% at one-year follow-up. This demonstrated that the less resource intensive group format was just as effective.

In a community clinic based in Australia, standard group delivery over 10 weeks was compared to a 2-week delivery of the same sessions in a daily rather than weekly format. Measures of anxiety and depression, as well as conduct, hyperactivity, and peer problems all reduced significantly ($p < .01$) from pre to post, while increasing strengths in several areas. Demonstrating that interventions across shorter time frames is also a plausible way of reducing barriers to engagement.

### Clinical Implications

Delivering effective CBT-based programs such as the FRIENDS programs in groups, shorter formats, and as preventative interventions in settings such as schools and lower socioeconomic areas, has the potential to reduce the barriers to engagement and reduce the gap in unmet mental health difficulties among children and adolescents.

### Future Directions

As CBT-based interventions continue to progress they will need to continue to adapt to the barriers that hinder their reach, efficiency, and effectiveness. Providing accessible treatment and preventive interventions to more young people remains a large challenge, research validating alternative ways of delivering these is essential. Furthermore, there remains a gap in the literature to investigate how different ways of delivering interventions impact on the availability and reach of these interventions and how effective modifications in format are at addressing barriers to engagement.

## Further Readings

Fisak, Jr, B.J., Richard, D., & Mann, A. (2011). The prevention of child and adolescent anxiety: A meta-analytic review. *Prevention Science, 12*(3), 255–268. doi:10.1007/s11121-011-0210-0

Gallegos-Guajardo, J., Ruvalcaba-Romero, N., Langley, A., & Villegas-Guinea, D. (2015). Selective prevention for anxiety and resilience promotion: Outcomes of an anxiety prevention and resilience program with girls at risk. *Pensando Psicología, 11*(18).

Stallard, P., Skryabina, E., Taylor, G., Phillips, R., Daniels, H., Anderson, R., & Simpson, N. (2014). Classroom-based cognitive behaviour therapy (FRIENDS): a cluster randomised controlled trial to Prevent Anxiety in Children through Education in Schools (PACES). *The Lancet Psychiatry, 1*(3), 185–192.

Chapter 5

# Interventions for school refusal and truancy: A case of 'old dogs in need of new tricks'?

David A. Heyne and Brandy R. Maynard

## Overview

School refusal and truancy are alike and different. Both are school attendance problems (SAPs) characterised by difficulty going to or staying in school. In school refusal the difficulty is associated with internalizing symptoms such as anxiety, mood problems, and physical complaints. The youngster — child or adolescent, male or female — is usually at home when not at school, and there is usually minimal emotional distress when attendance is not required (e.g., the weekend). Truancy, on the other hand, is an externalizing behaviour often paired with other externalizing behaviours such as fighting, stealing, and drug use. The youngster — commonly an adolescent male — may head to school but not arrive, or leave during the day, unbeknown to the parents. Difficulty attending may be associated with poor grades or the desire to fit in with truanting peers. Contextual factors (family, school, community) are also commonly discussed in relation to the development and maintenance of SAPs. Some risk factors are shared by school refusal and truancy while others are unique to one type of SAP. Because SAPs differ in form, associated risk factors, and the likely function served by non-attendance (e.g., avoiding emotional distress in school refusal; seeking more pleasurable activities in truancy), interventions for these two problems will also differ. The need for effective interventions is under-scored by the strong links between non-attendance, poor academic performance, social-emotional problems, and school drop-out.

## Major Findings

Behavioural and cognitive-behavioural interventions (herafter cognitive-behaviour therapy [CBT]) for school refusal have received most research attention. Common elements across CBT protocols are graded exposure to school attendance, parent involvement, family communication and problem solving, between-session tasks, and school consulta-tion. Treatment is mostly delivered individually and not in groups. Authors of a recent quantitative synthesis using meta-analytic methods identified eight quality studies of psychosocial interventions, seven of which were CBT. Post-treatment outcomes across 435 school-refusing youth indicated that intervention was associated with a significant increase in school attendance. This result is encouraging but it is not the full picture; there was no significant change in anxiety levels by post-treatment. Furthermore, a recent quali-tative synthesis suggests that outcomes are particularly poor for older school-refusing youth, those with a chronic or severe problem, and those who are socially anxious. Experience suggests that it is the socially anxious school refusers who are usually older when referred and who present with a more chronic and severe school refusal history. 'Old dog CBT' as currently implemented is clearly inadequate for this group. 'Old dog medication' has a longer history in the treatment of school refusal but two recent studies suggest that the newer medications such as fluoxetine do not enhance the effectiveness of CBT.

Truancy interventions tend to be fairly diverse and truanting youth are often 'treated' across a variety of settings and professions. CBT is used but less commonly than with school-refusing youth. In a systematic review and meta-analysis of indicated truancy interventions, 5 of 16 studies assessed the effects of an intervention with a CBT component. The CBT interventions ranged from a brief group intervention to interventions using contracting and incentives/rewards. Overall, findings indicated that interventions with chronic truant youth were effective, but CBT was not found to be any more or less effective than other interventions such as non-CBT therapy, court proceedings, or mentoring. Because truanting youth are a heterogeneous group, interventions such as CBT may result in differential effects across different types of truant youth. For example, a truant youth within the normative range for academic achievement and with little externalizing behaviour may respond differently to CBT than a truant youth presenting with low academic achievement and high levels of externalizing behaviour. Differential effects of truancy interventions have not been adequately examined.

## Clinical implications

Practitioners can have confidence in the likely benefits of CBT for school refusal when working with children. Interventions with adolescents, however, are likely to be longer due to severity and chronicity. Socially anxious school-refusing youth present a 'double dilemma': school non-attendance reduces opportunities to build social confidence.

Recommendations for this group have included supplementing individual CBT with group-based treatment or with pharmacological intervention, and placing greater emphasis on school-based interventions (e.g., reduced academic demands to compensate for the social demands of school; extra monitoring and support in relation to social exclusion). The need to involve parents in CBT for school refusal is unclear from an empirical viewpoint. Clinically, numerous authors suggest that parents be included in treatment as 'consultants, collaborators, and co-clients'. In a developmentally sensitive CBT, the parents of school-refusing adolescents can be helped to facilitate school attendance via a judicious combination of 'supportive' (autonomy-granting) and 'steering' (authoritative) strategies.

Practitioners working with truant youth can be confident about the likely benefits of intervening to improve attendance. However, the success of CBT, or any other intervention, may be contingent on the factors that are leading to the truant behaviour. It is recommended that practitioners assess individual, family, school, and community factors that may be contributing to non-attendance and implement an intervention with some evidence of efficacy around the factors driving the truancy. Behavioural contracting, providing incentives, and contacting parents about the youth's non-attendance are commonly used, easily implemented, and low cost interventions that have been found to work relatively well as an early intervention. Many youth, particularly those with more chronic truancy, may need more intensive interventions or additional intervention components based on the various risk factors present. For example, a truanting youth who has a substance use disorder and misses school to obtain or use substances may require an intervention to treat their substance use, whereas a youth who is skipping school due to feeling isolated and disengaged from school may benefit from interventions addressing their isolation and disengagement (e.g., CBT interventions; school-based mentoring).

## Future directions

Evaluation of early intervention for emerging SAPs is required, and interventions may differ for youth experiencing emotional distress (emerging school refusal) versus externalizing behaviour (emerging truancy). Treatment-wise, school refusal researchers are trialing extensions or variations of established CBT protocols (e.g., mindfulness; cognitive defusion techniques; dialectical behaviour therapy; psychoeducational exercise program). These 'new tricks' within the realm of school refusal interventions need to be evaluated in robust RCTs with long-term follow-ups. Additional moderation analyses can help determine the benefit of these innovations for sub-groups such as socially anxious school-refusing adolescents. Attempts are similarly being made to tailor interventions to truancy risk factors, building on accumulating literature on risk factors and heterogeneous profiles of truant youth. Family and school factors are likely very important in conceptualising and intervening in SAPs. While these factors have received attention in studies of risk for truancy, relatively little attention has been paid to these factors as risk for school refusal. In both fields, very little is known about how to most effectively intervene at the school and community level.

## Further Readings

Heyne, D.A., Sauter, F.M., & Maynard, B.R. (2015). Moderators and mediators of treatments for youth with school refusal or truancy. In M. Maric, P.J.M. Prins, & T.H. Ollendick (Eds.), *Moderators and mediators of youth treatment outcomes* (pp. 230–266). Oxford, England: Oxford University Press.

Maynard, B.R., Heyne, D., Brendel, K.E., Bulanda, J.J., Thompson, A.M., & Pigott, T.D. (2015). Treatment for school refusal among children and adolescents: A systematic review and meta-analysis. *Research on Social Work Practice*, doi: 10.1177/1049731515598619.

Maynard, B.R., McCrea, K.T., Pigott, T.D., & Kelly, M.S. (2013). Indicated truancy interventions for chronic truant students: A Campbell systematic review. *Research on Social Work Practice*, *23*, 5–21. doi: 10.1177/1049731512457207

Chapter 6

# Effects of bullying victimization on mental health outcomes in Australian youth

Sally Fitzpatrick and Kay Bussey

## Overview

Bullying victimization is a significant problem for children and adolescents in Australian schools. It has attracted considerable attention in the media over the past few years and there is growing evidence linking bullying to a range of poor mental health, social-emotional, and behavioural outcomes. Bullying is a complex social phenomenon that requires greater understanding of the risk and protective factors that exist at individual, school, family, and community levels. To date, universal intervention programs targeting a reduction in bullying victimization, and the associated negative consequences, have demonstrated limited success. Therefore, researchers are increasingly focused on the development of evidence-based programs targeting specific risk factors associated with bullying victimization. To establish the efficacy of such targeted programs, empirical evaluation of these programs alone, and in combination with whole-of-school approaches, is warranted.

## Major Findings

School bullying has detrimental effects on children and adolescents worldwide. Bullying is defined as a subset of aggressive behaviour that is characterised by the intentional and repeated harm of a powerless person(s). These harmful behaviours may be physical (e.g., hit, kicked), verbal (e.g., teased, called names), relational (e.g., rumours, negative gossip), or occur online (i.e., cyber-bullying). Bullying is typically characterised as a group process that occurs in a social context. Members of the peer group may engage in multiple roles including perpetrators, targets, supporters of the bully's behaviour, passive bystanders, or defenders of the victimized child. The focus of this review is on children who are targets of bullying behaviours. In Australia, approximately one third of young people report being bullied and up to 15% experience repeated and frequent victimization. Verbal and relational bullying is most commonly experienced by students. Traditional forms of bullying (physical, verbal, relational) have been shown to begin as early as pre-school, peak during the late primary and early high school years, and decline by the end of high school. In comparison, cyberbullying increases in mid-adolescence, as greater access to technology and engagement with social media enables students to extend their social interactions to the cyber world.

The antecedents and consequences associated with school bullying are well established. Research indicates that children are more likely to be bullied when they are submissive (anxious, insecure, sensitive) or react provocatively in the face of bullying. Non-behavioural characteristics that result in children standing out from their peers have also been associated with increased bullying (e.g., children who identify as lesbian, gay, bisexual, transgender, queer/questioning (LGBTQ), obese or disabled youth, children who are not liked or have low status in the peer group). The consequences of victimization includes internalizing distress and suicidal ideation; loneliness; externalizing behaviours, including increased substance use; relationship difficulties; lower self-esteem; physical illness; and poorer academic functioning. The bidirectional nature of these risk factors contribute to the vicious cycle of peer victimization over time. For example, research indicates that children who are bullied not only experience internalizing distress but may be further targeted as a result of how they manage this distress.

Not all children however, experience the same negative effects as a consequence of bullying, nor do they experience the same level of distress. Although some students experience few difficulties, for other children the negative effects of peer victimization may have long-lasting effects. This variability in outcome has led researchers to investigate how individual vulnerability may be moderated by individual (e.g., coping strategies, self-efficacy beliefs) and social (e.g., interpersonal relationships) protective factors which are amenable to intervention.

The primary focus of intervention research has been on school-based programs, which have met with limited success. As a consequence, researchers have begun to investigate multi-tiered systems of intervention in which universal and targeted programs combine to address school bullying. Universal school-based programs not only provide education for all children in the social group, but address the broader culture and climate of bullying within school and home environments. In comparison, targeted interventions aim to reduce victimization by addressing individual factors associated with victimization (e.g., anxiety, depression, anger, substance use). The role of targeted programs is not to stigmatise or blame children for being victimized, but to provide an individual focus alongside school-based initiatives. To date, there has been little empirical evaluation of multi-tiered approaches, or of individual targeted programs, to establish if these approaches provide effective forms of intervention.

## Clinical Implications

Targeted approaches to bullying require the development of specific programs for victimized children. Cognitive-behaviour therapy (CBT) programs that involve strategies to enhance social-skills, challenge negative cognitions (e.g., self-blame and acceptance of the bullying message), manage internalizing symptoms, reduce externalizing behaviours (e.g., substance use), and build adaptive coping strategies for dealing with the bullying, may be used in this context. However, few evidence-based CBT programs are available for clinicians working with victimized children. Examples of emerging CBT programs contextualised for bullying victimization and developed by Australian researchers include: *Confident Kids* and *Cool Kids — Taking Control*, both of which are aimed at victimized children with elevated levels of anxiety; and *Preventure*, a newly developed brief personality-targeted intervention for adolescent substance users which has been effective in reducing bullying victimization.

## Future Directions

Research on bullying victimization over the past few decades has made substantial strides in increasing understanding of the antecedents and consequences for peer victimization. However, bullying continues to be a major social problem affecting children in schools. Continued investigation into the risk factors that contribute to victimization, and the processes that maintain this complex social phenomenon, are required. Findings from this research should guide the development and evaluation of targeted interventions that address both risk and protective factors of peer victimization. Targeted programs are likely to not only enhance the efficacy of whole-of-school programs but also provide a useful stand-alone resource in clinical settings.

## Further Readings

Juvonen, J., & Graham, S. (2014). Bullying in schools: The power of bullies and the plight of victims. *Annual Review of Psychology, 65*, 159–185. doi:10.1146/annurev-psych-010213-115030

Wu, L., Zhang, D., Su, Z., & Hu, T. (2015). Peer victimization among children and adolescents: A meta-analytic review of links to emotional maladjustment. *Clinical Peadiatrics, 54*, 941–955. doi:10.1177/0009922814567873

Chapter 7

# Innovations in CBT for young people: Improving access and outcomes for vulnerable youth

Irene Sclare and Daniel Michelson

## Overview

Adolescents have been described as a 'forgotten group' with significant and distinctive health needs, often caught between service frameworks designed for younger children and adults, especially in the mental health arena. Most mental health problems start before aged 14, yet fewer than one quarter of adolescents with diagnosable psychiatric disorders receive appropriate help in the United Kingdom (UK) and Australia. Consequently, families, community agencies and commissioners have requested new service models that surmount existing structural and attitudinal barriers, and expand their range and scope.

Here, we highlight three innovations that are firmly rooted in the developmental capabilities, social contexts and help-seeking preferences of troubled teenagers. We will focus on: (1) DISCOVER, developed in London, UK, by Irene Sclare and colleagues at South London and Maudsley NHS

Foundation Trust; (2) HORYZONS, created by Mario Alvarez-Jiminez and colleagues at the National Centre of Excellence in Youth Mental Health, in Melbourne, Australia; and (3) Keep Composed, devised by Danielle Einstein at the Centre of Emotional Health at Macquarie University in Sydney. We argue that such age-appropriate interventions, founded on the best available evidence and theory, with substantial co-design input from young people, can deliver more accessible, acceptable and effective youth mental health care.

## Major Findings

DISCOVER has been developed in the UK to provide school-based support for 16 to 18 year olds with emergent emotional difficulties. The intervention uses a group workshop format that is facilitated by psychologists in a single day (6 hours) at a host school. DISCOVER incorporates an open-access, self-referral route as well as a teacher-assisted referral pathway. In this way, teachers can encourage vulnerable students to access help, but the final decision is made by the student.

The specification of DISCOVER was adapted from an established 'wellbeing workshop' model devised by June Brown for working age adults, then reviewed and refined with young people in an initial proof-of-concept study. The latest iteration incorporates new age-appropriate video material, a more interactive format and additional methods for personalisation and telephone follow-up by workshop facilitators. Particular attention is given to personal, relationship and academic stresses typical for the age group, while change strategies reflect adolescents' preferences for brief, practical and problem-solving approaches. DISCOVER created a partnership with a Teenage Adviser Group of vulnerable teenagers who worked with the team to shape and refine the clinical material, publicity and recruitment methods.

HORYZONS is an online social therapy that promotes long-term recovery in first episode psychosis. Its elements include peer-to-peer social networking, individually tailored psychosocial interventions and professional expert- and peer-moderation. It capitalises on the internet revolution's influence on access information and communication and the way in which young people interact. It was devised by an expert multidisciplinary panel and stakeholders to be a flexible early intervention. The model targets participants with psychosis in a safe online environment in which they can self-disclose, access peer support, learn about their disorder and be supported to receive therapeutic modules on managing specific mental health problems.

Keep Composed is one of a series of innovative trans-diagnostic programs developed by Dr Einstein and colleagues at Macquarie to enhance secondary school students' emotional and social competences and treat anxiety and depression symptoms. It was devised in collaboration with teachers to reduce worry and increase motivation in school students, and provide understanding and skills to respond to uncertainty. Dr Einstein has also helped develop Chilled Plus, an internet-based CBT program that includes a parent component; and the Insights program, which draws on theoretical and empirical studies in the areas of mindfulness, acceptance, perfectionism, procrastination, resilience and adolescent health.

## Clinical Implications

Community-based programs can become detached from mainstream mental health delivery, in part to enable them to be innovative and more accessible. Questions of clinical safety are important to consider, especially where there is little or no individual assessment. Alvirez-Jiminez and his colleagues designed HORYZONS to be a safe online service, with the capacity for very vulnerable young people to transition to specialist care within their larger system of services. DISCOVER undertakes risk management, and signposting to specialist care as required, for very troubled participants, without this prejudicing its open-access recruitment, and stigma-free approach. There are obvious requirements for staff clinical training, supervision and support within innovative projects, maintenance of good working links with the mainstream for service transitions.

Research into the therapeutic processes of an innovative program helps identify the key therapeutic change factors, thus enabling interventions to be clinically effective. Einstein and colleagues have set an impressive example for other program innovations in undertaking research into the importance of tackling intolerance of uncertainty (IU) in Keep Composed. While this level of enquiry into the nature of the therapeutic process has not as yet been formally evaluated in DISCOVER, its use of a goal-based approach, drawn from the model of its adult progenitor was investigated. Participants interviewed by a qualitative researcher stated they had appreciated the goal setting and telephone support but sought age-appropriate adaptations.

Importantly, the above-mentioned programs were developed with extensive user involvement and feedback. This offers the potential for major new insights and advances, guiding the service transformation away from relatively inaccessible and expensive clinic-based models and towards more acceptable and efficient models.

**Future Directions**

Randomised controlled trials (RCTs) are rightly regarded as 'gold standard' in determining whether new interventions are effective. Yet to fully judge program impact, in addition to mental health outcomes, we need reliable methods of evaluating programs on the basis of vocational and relational factors that sustain adolescents' recovery and wellbeing.

These three programs are designed to be relatively easy to implement in different contexts. High quality staff training needs to be available to ensure this. To assist effective dissemination, effective innovations should be embedded in mental health economies, without losing their integrity and focus, and included in mental health commissioning and funding. Finally, the three programs that we have described here use modern, developmentally appropriate methods to engage adolescents to manage adverse real life situations. To stay relevant to the age group, all such programs need to undergo regular reviews to ensure their method, content and design remain appealing and contemporary.

## Further Readings

McGorry, P, Bates, T., & Birchwood, M. (2013). Designing youth mental health services for the 21st Century: examples from Australia, Ireland and the UK. *British Journal of Psychiatry, 202,* s30–s35.

Fazel, M., Hoagwood, K., Stephan, S., & Ford, T. (2014). Mental health interventions in schools in high income countries. *The Lancet Psychiatry, 1,* 377–87

*Spreading and sustaining good ideas in health care* (2004). Innovations briefing: Department of Health publication. England.

## Chapter 8

# Innovative approaches to preventing and reducing substance use and mental health problems

Nicola C. Newton, Maree Teesson, Lexine Stapinski, Yael Perry, Fiona Shand, and Helen Christensen

## Overview

Anxiety, depression and substance use disorders are common and account for three quarters of the disability attributed to the mental disorders. To reduce the occurrence and cost of such disorders, effective prevention is critical. Although an array of prevention strategies exist, their effectiveness is often limited by barriers to implementation and sustainability. New innovative approaches are clearly needed to overcome traditional obstacles and reduce the significant burden of disease and social costs attributed to mental disorders. This chapter outlines a number of cutting edge research studies that are beginning to address the knowledge gaps and provide evidence for why we should focus on prevention and early intervention.

## Major findings

School-based programs to prevent alcohol and other drugs have been notoriously difficult to implement. Two recent programs have demonstrated promising effects and the potential for more effective implementation. Climate Schools is an online universal prevention program, designed to be delivered to all students, regardless of level of risk for developing substance use problems. The program was developed in Australia and has been evaluated in Australia and the United Kingdom (UK). It is based on social learning theory and uses cartoon storyboards to engage students and maintain interest. Its online format guarantees complete and consistent delivery and no teacher training is required. In contrast, Preventure is a selective personality-targeted intervention based on CBT principles and is delivered to students who are at increased risk of developing substance use problems. Preventure is brief yet highly structured with an accompanying manual and delivered by trained health professionals. Students screening as high-risk on one of four personality profiles (anxiety sensitivity, hopelessness, impulsivity and sensation seeking) are invited to participate in the brief personality-targeted interventions.

The effectiveness of both programs has been demonstrated in multiple trials, with results indicating students who received the Climate Schools or Preventure programs to be at reduced risk of consuming alcohol, binge drink and experience alcohol-related harms up to two years following the interventions, relative to those students who receive drug education as usual.

Despite older adolescence and young adulthood being a particularly high-risk time for alcohol and drug use, most prevention trials have a limited follow up period. One program that has recently demonstrated long-term impact among high-risk students is the selective personality-targeted Preventure program. Relative to high-risk control students, high-risk students who received the Preventure interventions displayed significantly lower risk of consuming alcohol, binge drinking, or experiencing alcohol-related harms over a 3-year period. In addition, preliminary results suggest that receiving Preventure also reduced growth in conduct problems, hyperactivity, symptoms of depression, anxiety, and overall psychological distress over the long-term follow up.

Online trials for prevention of depression are also growing. The Trial for the Prevention of Depression (TriPoD), is the first trial of a universal depression prevention intervention delivered to school students in advance of a specific, significant stressor. The TriPoD study aims to investigate the impact of SPARX-R, an online gamified intervention based on cognitive behavioural principles, on the prevention of depression in secondary school students prior to their final exams. The program is delivered online over the course of approximately seven weeks during school hours.

A recent trial, demonstrated that SPARX-R was effective in reducing depression symptoms, as measured by the Major Depression Inventory (MDI), at post-test and at 6 months relative to the control condition. Among participants with elevated depression at baseline (MDI > = 14), SPARX was effective at post-test and 6 months, while for those with lower depression scores (MDI < 14), the program significantly reduced depression symptoms at post-test only. Completion of at least four modules of the SPARX-R program was associated with significant effectiveness at post-test and follow-up, relative to control. Results indicate that an online, gaming intervention may offer schools a new approach to prepare students for their final year of schooling; however, issues pertaining to the feasibility and acceptability of the intervention must be resolved before wide scale dissemination is warranted.

With the rapid uptake of technology in Aboriginal and Torres Strait Islander communities, an opportunity exists to engage young people who are at risk of suicide. Self-reported reasons for not seeking help include: being too busy, too long to wait for an appointment, disliking the service or feeling embarrassed, and problems with transport. The iBobbly app, which aims to reduce suicidal thinking and psychological distress among young Aboriginal Australians, was developed in collaboration with several Indigenous communities. It may address many of these help-seeking barriers.

A recent pilot trial using a six-week waitlist control condition was conducted in the Kimberley, Western Australia. Outcomes were suicidal thinking, psychological distress, depression, and impulsivity. At baseline, participants reported severe psychological distress and moderately severe depression. Two-thirds reported having suicidal thoughts in the previous two weeks. At six weeks post-intervention, the iBobbly intervention group had significantly lower scores for depression and psychological distress, with a non-significant difference in suicidal thinking. There were no differences in impulsivity. Using technology to deliver therapy in an Aboriginal community was found to be feasible and acceptable. iBobbly shows promise in reducing depression and psychological distress, and may have an impact on suicidal thinking and behaviours.

## Clinical Implications

Evidence is emerging around the use of innovative approaches and new technologies to prevent substance use and mental disorders. Specifically, online universal interventions, selective CBT-based personality interventions and apps for indigenous populations are demonstrating significant prevention effects, offering educators and clinicians easy to implement and sustainable strategies to prevent and reduce substance use and mental disorders.

## Future Directions

Further research is needed to understand the mechanisms by which these interventions are resulting in change and independent replication trials are desirable.

## Further Readings

Champion K.E., Newton N.C., Barrett E.L., & Teesson, M. (2013). A systematic review of school-based alcohol and other drug prevention programs facilitated by computers or the internet. *Drug and Alcohol Review, 32,* 115–123.

O'Dea, B., Calear, A., & Perry, Y. (2015). Is e-health the answer to gaps in child and adolescent mental health service provision? *Current Opinion in Psychiatry, 28,* 336–342.

Newton, N.C., Conrod, P.J., Slade, T., Carragher, N., Barrett, E.L., Kelly, E., … Teesson, M. (2016). The long-term effectiveness of a selective, personality-targeted prevention program in reducing alcohol use and related harms: A cluster randomised controlled trial. *Journal of Child Psychology and Psychiatry.* doi: 10.1111/jcpp.12558

Chapter 9

# 'Screen time' and pathological technology use: Innovations in conceptualising and treating problems

Gerri Minshall and Daniel King

## Overview

Conceptualising and treating problematic technology use is a new and exciting frontier for cognitive-behavioural research and practice. This seems to be a particular area of interest for adolescent clinicians and researchers from all over the world. But seemingly ultra-modern problems with internet gaming or adolescents' excessive social media use can be informed and improved by awareness of older research into the impact of screen time. This traditional body of work investigated the impact of television and found profound effects of screen time on child and adolescent body mass index (BMI). A great deal of research is becoming concerned with the impact of screens and technology on sleep. Particularly helpful is Australian research that describes and maps problematic technology use and the behavioural, health and cognitive components of that presentation.

## Major Findings

Considering the scientific literature on the impact of the amount of screen time (usually defined as television and video viewing) points us to strong evidence of a positive correlation between the amount of screen time and child/adolescent BMI. There is cross sectional, experimental and longitudinal evidence that the more screen time, the fatter the child. The Dunedin study was able to hold constant important co-variates such as parental BMI, previous child BMI and socioeconomic status. Time spent watching TV predicts BMI and childhood viewing is a significant predictor of adult BMI at age 32. In a study conducted as early as 1999, Year 3 and Year 4 students who received an intervention around reducing television and video time (and who did so) were less likely to be obese a year later. Screen time is considered a hugely important driver in paediatric obesity and is a separate construct to physical activity. In the flurry of more newsworthy speculation on matters such as whether the internet changes your brain, we can forget that the basic impact on physical health (via BMI) is more relevant than ever.

There is epidemiology-style research not often considered by cognitive-behaviour therapists that seeks to clarify the link between mental health problems and screen time use. An epidemiological study conducted in the Netherlands sought to answer whether sedentary behaviour (television watching and computer use) were associated with anxiety and depressive disorders. Even when physical activity and socio-demographics were controlled for, people with Major Depressive Disorder spend more time using the computer. Sufferers of dysthymia, panic disorder and agoraphobia spend significantly more time each day watching television than controls. This study concluded that people with a mental health disorder spend more time in sedentary behaviour. There is also a dearth of how screen time may support and maintain various mental health diagnoses. Experienced clinicians often have a good feel for this but the word 'internet' is barely mentioned in the DSM-V.

But today the landscape *is* more complicated and ever-changing. For example, there are many more screens or forms of technology that allow humans to do different things such as socialise or game. The iPhone was first introduced to Australia in 2007. The second author (DK) has a body of work that describes pathological or harmful technology behaviours, maps how common these are in adolescents, differentiates what is problematic and what 'everyone' does and seeks to describe the underlying behaviour and cognitions. It was found that around 3% of Australian adolescents met criteria for pathological technology use (PTU) with gaming being more common for boys and using the internet more common for girls. The most time consuming electronic media use involved the internet (which included online social media). Adolescents more prone to problematic technology use also went to bed later.

There is also the big construct of parenting and how different parenting approaches may mediate all of these effects. It has been investigated that parental monitoring of screens (i.e., what is my child doing online and for how long) can be quite different to general parental monitoring (e.g., knowing where my child or adolescent is).

### Clinical Implications

The mostly paediatric research is the foundation of time-based guidelines and behavioural strategies to cut the amount of usage. For example, two hours of recreational use is recommended by the American Academy of Pediatrics for physical health. This literature contains many behavioural interventions such as 'stimulus control' (e.g., removing screens from bedrooms), parental monitoring (in terms of devices and amount of time) and the use of 'electronic shut downs'. Children and adolescents can be also asked to generate other things to do or define what a 'television zombie' is like. Not surprisingly, a meta-analysis into behavioural techniques that effectively reduce screen time found electronic shut downs to be the best.

Newer research more clearly defines what a clinical problem looks like and seeks to understand maintaining beliefs around problems such as excessive gaming. Other studies look at what people are actually doing on social media (e.g., social comparison, image management) and how these particular thoughts and behaviours might impact them. If cognitive-behavioural interventions more specifically target these maintaining factors then they will presumably be more effective.

There has been one successful randomised controlled trial (RCT) into group cognitive-behaviour therapy (CBT) for internet addiction in adolescents. This joint Australian-Chinese study yoked a parent group to a school-based intervention. Procedures focused on 'controlling your impulses' and 'recognising when addictive behaviour is occurring'.

A more general clinical implication is to include basic screen time/technology assessment questions into standard cognitive-behavioural assessments for children, adolescents and adults. Is technology use/screen time worthy of being part of the cognitive-behavioural formulation and furthermore should what we know about screen time be included in psycho-education or even clinician self-care?

## Future Directions

We often assume that assessment and treatment of screen time or technology use is something that desperately needs to be inflicted on adolescents. Yet BMI and the behaviours that underlie it (such as screen time habits) have been found to track from adolescence into adulthood. Intergenerational research into usage patterns between parents and their children is badly needed. Likewise what are the positive parenting practices around technology? Is co-gaming a good thing or a bad thing and why?

Linked to the point above, is that we do not know enough about risk and protective factors for pathological use.

How do typical mental health presentations use screen time and what should our key clinical recommendation be? Are these different for depressed or anxious clients or adolescents who are engaging in online socialising? Essentially, we don't know how similar our treatments should be for different presentations. Until this is clarified we suggest sticking with basic guidelines and continue to recommend the use of electronic 'shut downs'.

## Further Readings

King, D.L., Delfabbro, P.H. Zwaans, T., & Kaptsis, D. (2013). Clinical features and Axis I comorbidity of Australian adolescent pathological internet and video-game users. *Australian and New Zealand Journal of Psychiatry, 47,* 1058–1067.

De Wit, L., van Straten, A., Lamers, F., Cuijpers, P., & Penninx, B. (2011). Are sedentary television watching and computer use behaviors associated with anxiety and depressive disorders? *Psychiatry Research, 186,* 239–243.

Robinson, T. (1999). Reducing children's television viewing to prevent obesity: A randomized controlled trial. *The Journal of the American Medical Association, 282,* 1561–1567.

# Section 2

# Anxiety and Its Disorders

Chapter 10

# Broadening the research areas on social anxiety disorder

Junwen Chen, Erica Crome, Sarah Cox, Yulisha Byrow, Yoshihiro Kanai, Kristy Johnstone, Ryan Balzan, Lorna Peters, Quincy Wong, Andrew Baillie, and Stefan Hofmann

## Overview

Social Anxiety Disorder (SAD) is a highly prevalent mental disorder with far reaching negative consequences for overall functioning and wellbeing. Once coined the neglected anxiety disorder, research on social anxiety in the past decade has greatly increased, however many questions still remain. This chapter outlines progress towards answering some of these outstanding issues, presenting recent developments in social anxiety research. This includes an exploration of dispositional factors (i.e., evaluation fears and self-discrepancies) and cognitive biases (i.e., decision-making; attentional bias) to symptom maintenance and treatment outcomes in clinical and non-clinical populations. In addition, neural activity in socially anxious and non-anxious individuals during cognitive reappraisal is presented. Finally, we examined potential barriers influencing treatment-seeking behaviours in social anxiety.

## Major Findings

Dispositional factors feature strongly in the models of SAD. For example, fear of evaluation has been established as a core feature of SAD and recently, self-discrepancy has been named as the driving force of the disorder. As such, within the context of a speech task, we investigated self-discrepancies as a potential mechanism underlying evaluation fears in social anxiety and its related cognitive process, post-event rumination. In a sample of 99 undergraduate participants, multiple mediation analysis revealed that both ought-actual and feared-actual self-discrepancies influenced fear of negative evaluation, which in turn influenced state anxiety and post-event rumination. However, contrary to predictions, ought self-discrepancy did not influence fear of positive evaluation.

Cognitive theories propose that biased information processing also plays a central role in the development and maintenance of SAD. 'Jumping-to-Conclusions' (JTC) is a data-gathering bias characterised by hasty decision-making. This bias is typically linked to delusions or paranoia, but has also been found in people with high trait and state anxiety. To further explore the relationship between JTC and trait social anxiety and state anxiety, 186 undergraduate students were allocated to an anxiety-inducing manipulation or control condition, and classified as high or low socially anxious. All participants completed the 'beads task' to assess JTC, and the State-Trait Anxiety Inventory (state subscale) to assess state anxiety. Although the manipulation effectively induced state anxiety, there was no significant correlation between JTC and trait or state social anxiety. High socially anxious individuals showed more conservative decision making than controls, which may be an avoidance strategy.

Biased information processing can also impact on treatment outcomes for those with SAD. For example, studies have shown that individual differences in pre-treatment attention biases predict cognitive-behaviour therapy (CBT) outcome. However, whether vigilance towards threat predicts better or poorer treatment outcome is unclear. Therefore, we investigated the relationship between attention biases displayed by anxious individuals and CBT treatment outcome. Furthermore, we examined the influence of adult attachment style on this relationship. Individuals diagnosed with SAD, showing greater vigilance for threat at pre-treatment, were more likely to have poorer treatment outcomes than those that were avoidant of threat. In contrast, participants demonstrating greater difficulty disengaging from happy faces, compared to neutral faces, were significantly more likely to have poorer treatment outcomes. Attachment style did not moderate these relationships, however the interaction between anxious and avoidant attachment style independently predicted outcome.

Further concerning treatment for those with SAD, previous studies on cognitive reappraisal in social anxiety have shown the effects of reinterpretation of an emotion-eliciting stimulus on neural activities. Recent longitudinal research on cognitive reappraisal training revealed that one particular reappraisal strategy, psychological distancing, was more effective in reducing negative emotions than reinterpretation. As such, the effects of psychological distancing on neural activities during self-observation in individuals with social anxiety were investigated using functional magnetic resonance imaging (fMRI). High socially anxious participants and non-anxious controls watched their speech video in either a psychological distancing condition or control condition where participants were instructed to naturally respond to the stimuli. Neural responses in each condition were scanned by fMRI. Results indicated that non-anxious control group showed greater activation in the right orbitofrontal cortex during psychological distancing than high social anxiety group.

Another outstanding question is why a majority of people with SAD do not seek treatment, or do so after extensive delays. Barriers reported by people engaging in clinical services include fear of negative judgement, difficulties locating services and cost; yet little is understood about barriers experienced by non-treatment seeking samples. We assessed the relative importance of psychological, practical and economic barriers to accessing treatment for SAD in a sample of 2027 community participants. Outcomes confirmed the impact of fear of negative evaluation; and also identified fear of treatment failure, inconvenience and low willingness to pay out of pocket costs as additional treatment barriers deserving attention.

## Clinical implications

Overall, our results suggest that dispositional factors and biased information processing in social anxiety may play an important role in the development and maintenance of the disorder, and impact on treatment outcomes. Targeting these factors may enhance the effects of current treatments for SAD. For example, targeting self-discrepancies may reduce fear of negative evaluation, the core feature of social anxiety. Similarly, integrating strategies to modify attentional and decision-making biases may achieve better treatment outcomes. Furthermore, using indices of neuronal activity such as fMRI may produce a clearer understanding of various treatment effects on the phenomenological features of SAD. Finally, to increase engagement in treatment, service provision should acknowledge the financial difficulties and fear of treatment failure early in the treatment process.

## Future Directions

Further investigation of the interaction between dispositional factors and cognitive processes will enhance the overall understanding of SAD. To increase the efficacy of treatments for SAD, and to engage more consumers in treatment, future research should aim to replicate the findings reported here in diverse social settings and with clinical populations.

## Further Readings

Hofmann, S.G., & DiBartolo, P.M. (Eds.). (2014). *Social anxiety: Clinical, developmental, and social perspectives* (3rd ed.). Oxford, England: Elsevier/Academic Press.

Weeks, J.W. (Ed.). (2014). *The Wiley Blackwell handbook of social anxiety disorder.* Chichester, England: Wiley.

Chapter 11

# Evidence-based developments of CBT for late life anxiety

Naoko Kishita, Ken Laidlaw, Viviana M. Wuthrich, Sarah J. Egan, and Marie Chellingsworth

## Overview

Increased levels of life expectancy, beyond that achieved before in the history of mankind, is producing profound demographic change. As older people achieve previously unheard levels of longevity, they may require expert psychological input to maintain successful ageing in the face of age-related challenges. Equally, therapists working with older people may require guidance in applying evidence-based psychological treatments to maximise efficacious treatment outcomes. As people age, understanding an appropriate developmental context and frame of reference (e.g., applying gerontology rather than geriatric knowledge) for the treatment of common psychological conditions may become increasingly important to ensure suitable treatment goals are targeted and achieved. Anxiety disorders in later life, for instance provide a suitable class of conditions that may be experienced as qualitatively different from that of younger generations due to the types of challenges people face as they age (e.g., physical comorbidity, chronicity, loss experiences). Consequently, 'traditional' approaches to CBT may not always produce optimal outcome.

This chapter addresses whether the current psychological therapies workforce are prepared and able to meet potential challenges of working with much older cohorts. We provide a contemporary update of CBT for late life anxiety discussing how outcome may be enhanced by adopting age-appropriate interventions.

## Major Findings

Kishita and Laidlaw conducted a meta-analysis comparing the efficacy of CBT for generalised anxiety disorder (GAD) between older people and adults of working age. The study demonstrated that there were no statistically significant differences in the effect size of CBT for GAD between the two age groups. However, overall effect size was moderate for older people ($g = 0.55$) and large for adults of working age ($g = 0.94$), suggesting that there is still room for improvement in CBT with older people. The main difference in outcome between the two age groups was related to methodological quality in that no older people studies used an intention-to-treat design. Furthermore, the content analysis demonstrated that studies with older people were conducted according to robust CBT protocols but did not take account of gerontological evidence to make them more age-appropriate.

Wuthrich and her research team conducted a study comparing the effectiveness of group CBT to a discussion group for older adults with comorbid anxiety and depression. Participants were 133 older adults aged 60 to 88 with both an anxiety and unipolar mood disorder randomised to an 11-session CBT or discussion group. Both treatment groups resulted in significant improvements over time on all measures. At post-treatment, CBT produced significantly superior outcomes on diagnostic severity for the primary disorder, mean severity of all anxiety and mood disorders, total number of disorders present, and recovery rates, with non-significant differences on self-report measures of symptoms or wellbeing. However, at 6-month follow-up, differences between conditions were no longer significant. Therefore, group CBT produced faster and sustained improvements on diagnostic severity and recovery rates compared to an active control.

Egan and her research team examined group Mindfulness-Based Cognitive Therapy (MBCT) for people with Parkinson's disease in reducing anxiety and depression. Thirty-six participants with Parkinson's disease were randomly assigned to an 8-week MBCT group or waitlist control. The results indicated that at post-treatment there was a significant improvement in depression symptoms of large effect size in the treatment group compared to the waitlist control group. There was no effect on anxiety; however, participants had low levels of anxiety before the trial. Egan and her team are currently conducting a second trial of MBCT for anxiety and depression in Parkinson's disease that involves carers in mindfulness practice.

Chellingsworth explored the latest eight-year national data from the Improving Access to Psychological Therapies (IAPT) program with older people with depression and anxiety disorders in England. She addressed the current issues of the program, summarising that there is still considerable under-representation of older people among the population accessing the IAPT services. Chellingsworth et al. also present the results from their systematic review on low-intensity CBT with older adults. The application of low-intensity CBT may be exceptionally powerful in meeting the needs of an ageing population as these interventions equate to high-volume responses to need and may be the optimal approach to manage increasing demands and ensuring equality of access of older people given the profound demographic change affecting all nations.

## Clinical Implications

In some anxiety conditions (e.g., GAD) there is limited spontaneous remission and as such there will be longevity of conditions that may initially appear overwhelming to therapists inexperienced in applying CBT with older people. There is a need for age-appropriate interventions that make use of the competence, resilience and life-skills of older people to enhance treatment outcome.

Additionally there are some commonly held myths among health care professionals that older people are not interested in psychotherapies or psychological treatment does not work with older clients. The evidence demonstrated that both high-intensity CBT (e.g., individual face-to-face sessions) and low-intensity CBT (e.g., self-help guide) are effective for treating anxiety disorders among older clients.

## Future Directions

The aim of this chapter was to address a question whether the current clinical psychology workforce is prepared and able to meet the growing demands of older people. There is no doubt that further evidence-based developments of CBT in this area are crucial for achieving better outcomes. The data presented make it clear that more empirical research is needed to develop age-appropriate CBT interventions that directly and effectively address age-related challenges, such as complexity, comorbidity, and negative age biases to enhance treatment outcome. As older people have lived longer than their therapists they may have faced, and overcome, challenges not yet experienced by 'young' therapists. This is an important difference in the therapeutic dynamic in late life CBT. Any such age appropriate CBT intervention should seek ways to engage the life-skills of older clients.

## Further Readings

Laidlaw, K. (2015) *Cognitive behaviour therapy for older people: An introduction.* London, England: SAGE.

Karel, M.J., Gatz, M., & Smyer, M.A. (2012) Aging and mental health in the decade ahead: What psychologists need to know. *American Psychologist, 67*, 184–198.

Section 3

Obsessive Compulsive and Related Disorders

Chapter 12

# The self in psychological disorders: The example of obsessive-compulsive spectrum disorders

Daniel B. Fassnacht, Claire Ahern, Nathan Haymes, Adrienne Turnell, and Michael Kyrios

## Overview

Research on the self has led to a better understanding of psychological function and dysfunction. In particular, scholars increasingly highlight ruptures of the self in the understanding and treatment of psychological disorders. While there is an emerging literature on the importance of self across disorders, this chapter presents evidence from studies of self-construals in obsessive-compulsive spectrum disorders (OCSD) such as obsessive-compulsive disorder (OCD), body dysmorphic disorder (BDD) and hoarding disorder (HD). Self-constructs have been implicated in both the conceptualisation and diagnosis of psychological disorders such as OCD (e.g., the ego dystonicity of obsessions and compulsive behaviour in defining OCD). With the focus on the self, its ruptures and related constructs such as early schemas and attachment styles, practitioners and researchers have been able to enhance understanding of underlying mechanisms of psychological disorders (e.g., self-ambivalence in the etiology of OCD). Ultimately, by embedding the self into treatment and engagement formulations, practitioners might also be able to increase treatment acceptance by 'treating the person instead of the disorder' and, hence, advance the effectiveness of evidence-based interventions.

## Major Findings

Research about self-concepts has examined the *content* and *structure* of the self in relation to psychopathology. Studies focusing on content usually examine beliefs and appraisals about physical characteristics, personal attributes, as well as idiosyncratic expectations and goals. In OCD, ego-dystonic thoughts, images or impulses are, by definition, incongruent with one's self-views or values. For instance, Purdon and colleagues have found that the most upsetting intrusions are best distinguished from the least upsetting by the degree that they differ from one's sense of self. With respect to the content of values, individuals with OCD, relative to anxious and healthy controls, have been found to be more sensitive to issues relating to achievement, morality and perfectionism. There is also strong empirical evidence that, especially in OCSD, constructs such as high moral standards, a pivotal sense of responsibility and perfectionistic tendencies play crucial roles both in the etiology and maintenance of obsessive-compulsive beliefs and symptoms.

In contrast, the structure of the self-concept relates to the integration of different facets of the self, such as cohesion, consistency, and clarity. A self-concept that lacks integration and is vulnerable to perceived threats is frequently observed in OCSD. Guidano and Liotti's model of self ambivalence suggests that due to early developmental experiences and ambivalent attachments, individuals prone to obsessionality are highly ambivalent in their beliefs about themselves (i.e., strong feelings of uncertainty originating from concurrently held opposing views of oneself as 'worthy' and 'unworthy' in specific domains). In an effort to compensate for this and defend one's positive sense of self, there is an adherence to specific behaviour patterns or attachment to objects.

Recent studies by our own group have supported aspects of this theoretical position. Ahern and colleagues showed that individuals with self-esteem that was contingent on high moral standards in the context of self ambivalence yielded the greatest OCD symptoms. Using a large-scale analogue community sample, Haymes and colleagues examined the relationship between insecure adult attachments (i.e., attachment anxiety and avoidance) and BDD symptom severity. The study revealed that the relationship between insecure adult attachment, especially attachment avoidance, and BDD severity could be explained by their self ambivalence even after controlling for depressive symptoms. In two separate studies, Kyrios, Mogan, Frost and colleagues found that developmental factors were associated with hoarding symptoms; in particular, amassing of possessions was associated with experiences of relative emotional deprivation (e.g., lack of warmth in family of origin). In one study assessing hoarding and OCD cohorts as well as healthy controls from the community, results indicated that recollections of lack of warmth in one's family was related to greater uncertainty about oneself and others which, in turn, predicted greater hoarding symptoms and saving cognitions while accounting for age and depressive symptoms.

While much research has been conducted using survey methodologies, some experimental research is also emerging in support of the importance of self-processes in OCD. Using an exposure experiment to simulate experiences of OCD-specific unwanted intrusions, participants were asked to respond to the intrusions by either neutralising or using refocusing techniques. Ahern and colleagues found that pre-task self-vulnerability was associated with lower self-worth and confidence during the neutralisation task, which in turn was associated with greater distress and the urge to neutralise. This is the first known study to experimentally test how vulnerable self-worth leads to more intense and aversive experiences when individuals are confronted with unwanted intrusions. Findings are consistent with cognitive models for the development of OCD, and lend support that examination of self-processes provides useful insights into our understanding and, potentially, treatment of such disabling disorders. The treatment implications are made more potent by Bhar and colleagues' recent finding that the resolution of self ambivalence predicted better treatment outcomes and lower rates of relapse in OCD patients.

## Clinical Implications

We argue that paying greater attention to the self as a therapeutic target opens a potential way of combining and reconciling various theoretical standpoints. In fact, the self already occupies a central position in the formulation of disorders across different theoretical paradigms, whether in the form of addressing attachment insecurities, dysfunctional self-schemas or using treatment techniques around self-based case formulations. We anticipate that interventions targeting self-processes will improve therapeutic outcomes and decrease relapses; 'treating the person instead of the disorder' could enhance both the quality of the therapeutic alliance, as well as treatment motivation and engagement.

## Future Directions

The self has great potential for enhancing our understanding and conceptualisation of psychological dysfunction. However, there is still much to do: First, we need a clearer operationalisation of 'the self' and consensus of which factors across the content and structure of the self relate to each other or are associated with specific symptom constellations. When common ground or a common language is found, longitudinal studies could examine etiological associations between self-processes and the emergence of dysfunctional symptoms. Second, experimental research needs to augment survey-based research in establishing causal links between self-processes and symptoms. Finally, future research should focus on the development and examination of the impact of self-based intervention strategies in the treatment of psychological disorders.

## Further Readings

Guidano, V., & Liotti, G. (1983). *Cognitive processes and emotional disorders.* New York, NY: Guilford Press.

Kyrios, M., Moulding, R., Doron, G., Bhar, S., Nedeljkovic, M., & Mikulincer, M. (2016) *The self in understanding and treating psychological disorders.* Cambridge, England: Cambridge University Press.

Kyrios, M., Nelson, B., Ahern, C., Fuchs, T., & Parnas, J. (2015). The self in psychopathology. *Psychopathology, 48,* 275–277.

Chapter 13

# Body dysmorphic disorder in children and adolescents: Advances in theoretical and clinical research

Sophie C. Schneider, Lara J. Farrell, Cynthia M. Turner, and Haley J. Webb

## Overview

Body dysmorphic disorder (BDD) is an obsessive-compulsive spectrum disorder that involves excessive preoccupation with perceived defects in appearance. BDD typically begins in early to mid-adolescence, and prevalence estimates suggest that it is almost as common as OCD, yet comparatively poorly understood. BDD can be severely debilitating in young people, involving high distress and functional impairment, poor insight, elevated comorbidity, and high suicidality. Though research into BDD during the child and adolescent years is limited, recent studies have provided insights into the importance of early detection, the need for effective developmentally appropriate interventions, and to have informed cognitive-behavioural models of BDD. This chapter will review current findings and future directions for research across these domains.

## Major Findings

The prevalence of BDD in young people is approximately 2%, but a range of factors contribute to poor disorder recognition. At least half of young people with BDD are convinced that their appearance concerns are realistic, and those that recognise their concerns as excessive are often reluctant to discuss these concerns with others. It can be difficult to understand the distress experienced by young people with BDD, especially as symptoms are often unobservable to others (e.g., obsessive thoughts about appearance) or may be performed in private (e.g., skin picking or mirror gazing).

Mental health professionals often fail to diagnose BDD. BDD concerns are rarely spontaneously disclosed to health professionals, even when they are the principal source of interference, highlighting the need to carefully screen for the presence of BDD in young people. Further, BDD is highly comorbid with depressive disorders, anxiety disorders, obsessive-compulsive disorder, eating disorders, and substance use disorders. As these disorders share some transdiagnostic features with BDD (such as low mood, persistent worry, excessive dieting and exercise, and repetitive checking behaviours), it is not uncommon to diagnose the comorbid disorder and miss the presence of BDD. In psychiatric populations, those with a diagnosis of BDD can be more severely unwell than those without, further emphasising the need for appropriate diagnosis.

Preliminary research into the treatment of BDD in young people indicates that cognitive-behaviour therapy (CBT) and pharmacotherapy (typically using serotonin reuptake inhibitors) can be effective. Expert clinicians have highlighted the need to tailor existing adult CBT treatments to the developmental stage of the individual, for example, by modifying the language and tasks in CBT manuals to suit the participant's age. Additionally, the level of family involvement in treatment should be decided based on the quality of family relationships, level of involvement by family members in BDD behaviours, and attitudes towards BDD. Motivation for treatment may be particularly low among young people, especially when insight into BDD is poor, potentially requiring a greater focus on contingency management and motivational interviewing. Finally, suicidality appears to be particularly high in youth BDD, so suicide risk should be closely monitored and managed, with consideration to the use of pharmacotherapy. There currently exists very limited research examining interventions for BDD in young people, so there is a great deal to be learned about effectively treating this complex disorder.

Cognitive behavioural models of BDD have identified a range of potential risk factors across biological (e.g., genetics, neurobiology), psychological (core beliefs, personality, cognitive processes) and social (negative childhood experiences, values about appearance) domains. However, these models are primarily informed by research with adults. Evaluating these models in young people during the time of peak BDD onset is likely to provide richer and more accurate findings. For example, a recent study found a bidirectional longitudinal association between adversity in peer relationships and BDD symptoms in young people. That is, not only did increased relational victimisation by peers predict higher BDD symptoms one year later, but BDD symptoms predicted declines in the perception of acceptance by peers over time.

## Clinical Implications

Identifying and treating BDD in young people represents a crucial opportunity to reduce the distress and impairment associated with this under-recognised disorder. BDD is typically not detected using standard clinical assessments, so specific probing or brief BDD screening tools should be adopted by clinicians. Questioning must be sensitive to the fact that the individual may be convinced that their concerns are justified. If possible, a multi-informant approach is recommended to provide additional information. Preliminary evidence suggests some promise for CBT and pharmacotherapy treatments in treating youth with BDD, though adaptations are required to suit the developmental stage and presenting characteristics of each client. Recommended treatment of BDD can be intensive (e.g., 12–22 sessions of CBT), though there is promising early evidence in adults that lower intensity internet-CBT may be appropriate for use with less severe BDD presentations. The evaluation and refinement of cognitive-behavioural models of BDD in youth may lead to new directions for clinical practice. In particular, a greater understanding of the individual vulnerabilities, precipitants and mechanisms underlying the onset and exacerbation of BDD symptomology will provide critical information that may enable richer and more effective methods of intervention and prevention.

**Future Directions**

Research into BDD among children and adolescents is in its infancy. Scientific knowledge is greatly needed across most key domains; population prevalence, clinical correlates, diagnostic sensitivity and specificity, enhancing treatment outcomes, and refining current models of BDD. Education of the public and mental health professionals is recommended in order to improve early detection and appropriate treatment of BDD. Despite these limitations, recent advances in the study of BDD in young people represent a growing recognition of the importance of this research during this crucial developmental period.

## Further Reading

Fang, A., & Wilhelm, S. (2015). Clinical features, cognitive biases, and treatment of body dysmorphic disorder. *Annual Review of Clinical Psychology, 11*, 187–212. doi:10.1146/annurev-clinpsy-032814-112849

Phillips, K.A. (2010). Pharmacotherapy for body dysmorphic disorder [Special Issue]. *Psychiatric Annals, 40*(7), 325–332.

Wilhelm, S., Phillips, K.A., & Steketee, G. (2013). *Cognitive-behavioral therapy for body dysmorphic disorder: A treatment manual.* New York, NY: Guilford.

Chapter 14

# Advances in cognitive behavioural models and treatments of trichotillomania (hair pulling disorder)

Imogen C. Rehm, Jade Walters, Reneta Slikboer, Tanya Arabatzoudis, Richard Moulding, Mark Boschen, and Maja Nedeljkovic

## Overview

Trichotillomania (TTM) involves the repetitive, uncontrollable removal of hair resulting in hair loss, typically from the scalp, eyebrows, and eyelashes. TTM affects more women than men; is associated with high rates of psychiatric comorbidity, disability, and distress; and often has a chronic trajectory. Once believed to be rare, the current consensus suggests that prevalence rates of 1% are likely to be underestimates. Despite the clear need for a comprehensive understanding of, and effective treatments for, TTM, it remains a poorly understood and under-researched disorder. The development of cognitive-behaviour therapy (CBT) for TTM has occurred in the past two decades in the absence of an integrated, evidence-based cognitive behavioural model of its onset and maintenance. This chapter provides an overview of the current cognitive behavioural models proposed of TTM, and highlights findings from new Australian research on the disorder. Ultimately, this research extends knowledge of the emotion regulation processes, and dysfunctional cognitions and beliefs implicated in TTM, and bolsters support for interventions that target these processes. Future directions to advance CBT research in TTM are proposed.

## Major Findings

Current models of TTM pay particular attention to behavioural and emotion regulation processes, while the relevance of cognitive processes in symptom onset and maintenance have largely been overlooked. The behavioural perspective suggests that TTM develops because of learned stimulus-response associations (via classical conditioning) and response contingency associations (via operant conditioning). Cues eliciting hair-pulling behaviour (e.g., feeling the texture of a coarse hair) can be identified and modified in treatment using practical strategies (e.g., making a clenched fist when experiencing the urge to pull). The behavioural perspective has been instrumental to the development of habit reversal therapy (HRT), which is currently regarded the frontline treatment of TTM. However, the behavioural model offers no explanation regarding why some individuals are susceptible to developing TTM.

On the basis that hair-pulling often occurs in response to negative affect (e.g., frustration, anxiety), an emotion regulation model was recently proposed, which suggests that individuals who develop TTM may be vulnerable to emotion dysregulation and engage in hair-pulling to regulate the intensity and expression of their emotions (see Further Readings). Indeed, we have found that hair-pulling severity was positively associated with emotion dysregulation, experiential avoidance (i.e., the attempt to avoid unpleasant experiences, thoughts, and emotions), and distress intolerance. Furthermore, emotion dysregulation and distress intolerance were significantly poorer among individuals who endorsed hair-pulling behaviours than in those who did not, over-and-above depressive symptoms.

While a cognitive model of TTM (based upon a cognitive model of substance abuse) was proposed 20 years ago, it appears to have inspired little research into exactly what — if any — dysfunctional cognitions and beliefs contribute to TTM. Cognitive techniques have nevertheless been introduced to behavioural therapies for TTM, but on the basis of limited evidence. Using qualitative research methods (see Further Readings), we identified several maladaptive cognitions and beliefs associated with TTM, of which, one has demonstrated particular importance; negative self-beliefs. Extending these qualitative findings, our preliminary analyses of online survey data suggest that negative self-beliefs significantly predict TTM symptom severity, even after controlling for depression and emotion regulation processes. Self-perceptions may be a pertinent factor to address in CBT for TTM, although this suggestion requires investigation.

In a qualitative paper evaluating a three-day peer-support program for TTM, we also found that participants identified several cognitive factors that they believed contributed to subjective symptom improvements post-program. By challenging participants' perceptions that they were 'the only one' with, and ostracised due to, their experience of TTM, participants developed a new narrative around their disorder in which they belonged to a unique, supportive, and understanding community of people 'like them'. Ultimately, reducing participants' sense of social ostracism allowed their exploration of emotions associated with TTM and their receptiveness to learning strategies during the program that were intended to reduce hair-pulling.

## Clinical Implications

Meta-analyses have shown that CBT produces greater symptom reduction than pharmacotherapy (see Further Readings). However, one quarter of treatment responders following CBT have been reported to relapse as early as one-month following treatment completion, indicating the need for further development and refinement of treatment approaches for TTM that are based upon an improved understanding of the disorder. At least two patterns of hair-pulling characterise TTM: (1) focused hair-pulling, which the individual intentionally performs in response to unpleasant emotions, sensations, and cognitions; and (2) automatic hair-pulling, which the individual performs with limited-to-no awareness, and often during sedentary activities. Whether these two hair-pulling patterns can be considered 'subtypes' requires ongoing research, but their distinction appears to have influenced the blending of behavioural therapies with interventions that provide alternative methods to cope with emotions and unpleasant internal states, such as acceptance and commitment therapy (ACT) and dialectical behaviour therapy (DBT).

These blended interventions have had promising treatment outcomes, reducing TTM symptom severity, and levels of emotion dysregulation and experiential avoidance at three months post-treatment. Such findings may be an indication that ACT and DBT alter the cognitive-affective mechanisms maintaining focused hair-pulling, in particular. However, the role of TTM subtypes has received limited attention in the treatment literature. Further research is required to identify whether treatment would be more effective in specifically targeting automatic and focused hair-pulling patterns, or to continue to treat the disorder with a 'one size fits all' approach.

## Future Directions

We believe that an integrated, evidence-based cognitive behavioural model of TTM will be essential for the continued development of effective therapies for TTM. Future research on the role of cognitive, self-regulatory, personality, and motivation-based processes in TTM — and how these differ according to possible disorder subtypes — will make a direct contribution regarding what components ought to be included in CBT for TTM. Internationally, experts are increasingly calling for such research, as well as for component-sequencing studies that identify the most effective elements of standard and third-wave CBTs in producing and maintaining behaviour change. Locally, it will be necessary that research efforts focus upon making effective treatments accessible for the estimated 200,000 or more Australians with TTM, be it through ongoing implementation of brief peer-support programs or the use of online technologies.

## Further Readings

Rehm, I. C., Nedeljkovic, M., Thomas, A., & Moulding, R. (2015). The role of cognitions and beliefs in trichotillomania: A qualitative study using interpretative phenomenological analysis. *Behaviour Change, 32*(4), 209–230. doi:10.1017/bec.2015.11

Roberts, S., O'Connor, K., & Bélanger, C. (2013). Emotion regulation and other psychological models for body-focused repetitive behaviors. *Clinical Psychology Review, 33,* 745–762. doi:10.1016/j.cpr.2013.05.004

Slikboer, R., Nedeljkovic, M., Bowe, S., & Moulding, R. (2015). A systematic review and meta-analysis of behaviourally based psychological interventions and pharmacological interventions for trichotillomania. *Clinical Psychologist.* doi:10.111/cp.12074

Section 4

Trauma, PTSD and Grief

Chapter 15

# Psychological mechanisms underpinning psychopathology in refugees

Belinda Liddell, Ola Ahmed, Rosanna Pajak, Emma Doolan, and Angela Nickerson

## Overview

The number of individuals displaced by war, conflict and persecution is now in excess of 60 million. Recipient countries are tasked with meeting the daily needs of refugees and asylum seekers, many of whom are struggling with the mental health consequences of exposure to severe human-rights violations. Furthermore, post-settlement adjustment-related stressors, such as family separation, financial difficulties and language barriers, can also undermine psychological wellbeing. These pre- and post-migration factors coalesce to have a significant impact on the mental health of refugees. Rates of posttraumatic stress disorder (PTSD) and depression are approximately 30% among refugees, which is five times the rate of these disorders in the populations of the host countries. Despite this, many refugees are psychologically resilient and adapt well post-displacement. As yet, there is little evidence elucidating the factors at play in determining these different adaptation pathways. Empirical research into the biological and psychological mechanisms that underpin refugee adaptation is therefore critical, and will inform the development of effective and efficient clinical treatments and services for refugees. Emerging evidence suggests that core mechanisms influencing psychopathology in refugees may include (1) heightened fear reactivity and deficits in fear processing; (2) dysregulated management of fear and other emotional responses; (3) sensitivity to injustice; and (4) reduced self-efficacy. Below we outline key findings in each of these domains to date, and discuss how these may influence the adaptation of refugees.

**Major Findings**

Advances in understanding the neural mechanisms underpinning posttraumatic stress disorder (PTSD) have resulted in PTSD being conceptualised as a stress-reactivity disorder, characterised by disrupted fear responsivity. It is unclear whether similar alterations to the neural dynamics of fear processing are apparent in refugees with PTSD, representing a major gap in the field. Many refugees have been exposed to prolonged interpersonal trauma, with over 20% of resettled refugees being survivors of torture. Torture can have profound and specific repercussions for both physical and psychological health. Evidence from non-refugee survivors of severe chronic violence such as childhood sexual abuse suggests that fear reactions in these groups may be characterised by emotional numbing and withdrawal, rather than the hypervigilant fear responses that define classic PTSD. Other studies suggest that survivors of war and torture display both hypervigilance and avoidance reactions to negative cues (see Further Reading). It is important to examine these mechanisms more closely in refugees and torture survivors in order to consider the multiple impacts of past trauma severity, current psychopathology and contextual stress on the neural systems of fear. Insights will have implications for designing psychological interventions that promote post-trauma adaptation among refugees.

Emotion dysregulation has been implicated in the development and maintenance of multiple psychological disorders, including PTSD. While this construct has been widely investigated with western clinical populations, the extent to which emotion dysregulation influences posttraumatic stress responses in refugees is largely unknown. There is emerging empirical evidence that difficulties regulating emotional responses mediate the association between trauma exposure and post-migration living difficulties, and psychological outcomes in a refugee sample (see Further Reading). This highlights the contribution of both pre-migration and post-migration contextual factors in influencing refugees' capacity to manage distressing emotions. To inform psychological interventions that target emotion dysregulation, it is also important to investigate which emotion regulation strategies are effective in reducing distress for refugees. Research with non-refugee trauma survivors has indicated that cognitive reappraisal is an adaptive emotion regulation strategy for individuals with PTSD, whereas suppression is linked with poor emotional outcomes including fear, anger, and distress. To date, however, there has been little empirical investigation of how effective these emotion regulation strategies are for refugees with traumatic stress symptoms. This represents an important avenue of enquiry that could directly inform treatment interventions for this group.

By definition, refugees and asylum seekers are exposed to persecution and violence in their countries of origin. These experiences are not only traumatic, but often represent salient examples of injustice. In addition, injustice is also an important feature of displacement and resettlement. Despite the salience of the concept of injustice to the refugee experience, little research has directly investigated how it contributes to mental health outcomes in this population. The broader injustice literature points to the significance of justice sensitivity, a trait representing how readily people perceive and react to injustice, in understanding the complex impact of injustice on mental health. Investigations with student populations have suggested that heightened justice sensitivity predicts attentional biases towards injustice cues, interpretation of ambiguous situations as unjust, and increased affective reactivity. Better understanding the impact of justice sensitivity on psychological and social functioning in refugee populations may provide important insights into the mechanisms by which injustice experiences influence mental health outcomes. Research advancing knowledge regarding the cognitive, affective and behavioural processes involved in justice sensitivity will importantly inform the ongoing development of clinical models relating to refugee mental health.

Reduced self-efficacy is a common characteristic of clinical populations, and research suggests that it is also related to psychopathology among refugee groups. Self-efficacy refers to an individual's belief in their capacity to organise and manage their goals, actions, behaviours and cognitions. In addition to the negative impact of traumatic events, the settlement experience can challenge many aspects of self-efficacy, as refugees are commonly unable to resume their professional lives, are separated from supportive family and community, and initially dependent on government welfare. In other populations, low self-efficacy has been linked with suicidal ideation and symptoms of clinical depression, both of which are high among resettled refugees. Understanding these relationships will provide a basis for advancing clinical strategies that enhance self-efficacy in refugee populations.

## Clinical Implications

The profound impact of the refugee experience on mental health poses significant challenges for clinicians working with refugees. Enhanced understanding of the basic psychological and neurobiological mechanisms that underlie the mental health of refugees will provide the building blocks for the development of effective psychological interventions for refugee clients. By developing targeted treatments that specifically address the mental health needs of refugees, clinicians will be better able to help refugee clients overcome the psychological effects of trauma and displacement.

## Future Directions

Empirical research is essential to develop the evidence base that will inform clinical models and to develop effective treatments to alleviate psychological suffering among refugees. Understanding the mechanisms underlying why some refugees adapt well while others develop psychological disorders is fundamental to informing service provision from both a mental health and settlement perspective.

## Further Readings

Nickerson, A., Bryant, R.A., Schnyder, U., Schick, M., Mueller, J., & Morina, N. (2015). Emotion dysregulation mediates the relationship between trauma exposure, post-migration living difficulties and psychological outcomes in traumatized refugees. *Journal of Affective Disorders, 173*, 185–192.

Nickerson, A., Bryant, R.A., Rosebrock, L., & Litz, B.T. (2014). The mechanisms of psychosocial injury following human rights violations, mass trauma and torture *Clinical Psychology: Science and Practice, 21,* 172–191.

Adenauner, H., Pinösch, S., Catani, C., Gola, H., Keil, J., Kißler, J., & Neuner, F. (2010). Early processing of threat cues in posttraumatic stress disorder — evidence for a cortical vigilance-avoidance reaction. *Biological Psychiatry, 68,* 451–458.

Chapter 16

# Traumatic events, cognitive processes, and the development of psychological interventions for youth

Anna McKinnon, R. Meiser-Stedman, S. Hogan, and Reg. D. V. Nixon

## Overview

Exposure to stressful experiences in childhood can lead to the development of posttraumatic stress disorder (PTSD) and a range of mental health conditions. PTSD is a debilitating psychiatric disorder affecting approximately 5% to 25% of children and adolescents exposed to single-incident traumas such as motor vehicle collisions and assaults. A sizeable proportion of this vulnerable population will also fulfil diagnostic criteria for a comorbid psychiatric disorder, including major depressive disorder and generalised anxiety disorder. These conditions lead to enduring disability, and the interference caused at this critical time during a child's life can influence their life course. The development of effective psychological interventions for these youth can counteract these problems, having the potential to set the stage for a healthy and productive life.

## Major Findings

Over the past 30 years, the body of theoretical research on the core clinical and cognitive phenotypes associated with the development of PTSD has expanded rapidly. There are several prospective studies which track the acute course of PTSD and related psychopathology in samples of children and adolescents recruited from hospital and emergency departments. Across these studies, sizeable recovery from PTSD in the first 2 to 3 months following a trauma has been reported. Studies also highlight the benefit of cognitive behavioural models, showing that the disorder presents itself in a manner consistent with adult-based models. Factors such as aspects of trauma memories, the meanings young people attach to their trauma, and the inappropriate management of symptoms (e.g., avoidance, thought suppression) are considered to be principal risk factors. There is also research addressing the neurobiological underpinnings of PTSD in youth; for example, there is support for the suggestion that enhanced emotional reactivity to reminders thought to reflect underlying dysregularity within systems associated with stress such as the hypothalamic–pituitary–adrenal axis is a feature of youth with PTSD.

In line with theoretical developments, several psychological interventions have been examined. Early intervention studies for youth delivered within one month of trauma have typically tested brief universal interventions that utilise a debriefing model or the provision of psychoeducation. These treatments have led to little improvement in PTSD symptoms for children. The most widely supported treatment for PTSD is individual trauma-focused cognitive behaviour therapy (TF-CBT), demonstrated to be effective as both an acute and chronic intervention for youth. There is marked variability in the effect sizes of TF-CBT programs, possibly due to some protocols testing packages where all patients receive the same fixed program and others testing modular and case-formulation driven treatments. A significant challenge currently is the low uptake of TF-CBT by clinicians in the community, with some clinicians questioning the relevance of TF-CBT to the young people they see in the community who have multiple diagnoses and complex presentations. There is also a general concern held by some therapists that carrying out processes such as imaginal or prolonged exposure could re-traumatise children. These barriers to implementation highlight need for trials evaluating the effectiveness of TF-CBT in community settings.

**Clinical Implications**

Progress in theorising over the past thirty years has led to the widespread support for individually delivered TF-CBT as the frontline treatment for PTSD in youth. In the coming years, more attention must be paid to the merits of family focused, group, self-help and internet TF-CBT paradigms as they may improve cost-effectiveness and facilitate access to care. The adoption of a trans-diagnostic approach to conceptualise responses to trauma could lead to a new generation of treatments for PTSD that focus on treating the transdiagnostic processes highly indicative of poor long-term outcomes. Finally, interventions such as dialectical behaviour therapy (DBT) and mindfulness-based cognitive therapy (MBCT) are thought to facilitate improved emotion regulation, and there is emerging support for these interventions in young people. Comparing CBT to third-wave interventions and pharmacological medications, or testing a combination of CBT with these treatments, could lead to enhanced outcomes, particularly for those children with complex presentations.

**Future Directions**

Several areas of research are needed to improve the breadth of treatment options available to traumatised youth. A greater focus on the role of family factors is needed. Establishing the acute course of dysregularity within neurobiological systems for children with PTSD is also crucial, which might support treatments combining TF-CBT with psychopharmacological medications. Research investigating computer-based attribution training may also provide important information in relation to interventions complementary to existing TF-CBT. Research investigating computer-based attribution training may also provide important information in relation to interventions complementary to existing TF-CBT. Findings from process-driven research with single incident trauma victims must be replicated with multiple trauma victims (e.g., neglect, repeated sexual abuse) as it is argued these sufferers are characterised by a distinct profile of PTSD symptoms (i.e., complex PTSD). Greater investigation of the factors unique to the Complex PTSD presentation is required; for example, profound emotion regulation problems and dissociative experiences. Finally, continued efforts are needed to understand the processes that increase the risk for comorbid problems as this trans-diagnostic approach could revolutionise theory and treatment of traumatic stress responses. The first step towards the development of such an approach involves elucidating the trans-diagnostic dimensional structure of trauma-related psychopathology and identifying the factors indicative of poor prognosis.

To summarise, despite significant improvements to the body of knowledge addressing the aetiology and psychological treatment of PTSD in youth, the choice of interventions for traumatised youth is still relatively limited relative to other disorders in youth. One of the most important areas in the coming years is support for interventions for youth with high levels of comorbidity and complex presentations.

## Further Readings

Smith, P., Perrin, S., Yule, W., & Clark, D.M. (2010). *Cognitive therapy for post-traumatic stress disorder.* London, England: Routledge Press.

Meiser-Stedman, R. (2002). Towards a cognitive-behavioral model of PTSD in children and adolescents. *Clinical Child and Family Psychology Review, 5,* 217–231. doi: 10.1023/A:1020982122107

National Collaborating Centre for Mental Health (2005). *Clinical Guideline 26. Post-traumatic stress disorder: The management of PTSD in adults and children in primary and secondary care.* National Institute for Clinical Excellence.

Chapter 17

# Understanding, screening and treating anger in posttraumatic stress disorder

Tony McHugh, David Forbes, Jacqueline Costello, David Said, Nathan Alkemade, and Richard Cash

## Overview

While most individuals exposed to potentially traumatising events will quickly recover equilibrium, a proportion develop serious posttraumatic mental health conditions, like posttraumatic stress disorder (PTSD). Further, although effective PTSD treatment(s) exist, a significant minority of sufferers fail to respond to treatment and instead develop a chronic form of the condition. This reflects (a) the incompatibility of anxiety-based models of PTSD with the more than 50 per cent of PTSD presentations where anger is prominent in its own right or in combination with other negative affects; and (b) the limiting or interfering impact of anger on PTSD treatment. Anger's critical role is well documented in research of combat-related PTSD, increasingly so among contemporary military personnel. It is important to note, nevertheless, that anger dysregulation is a significant problem among diverse populations. Given anger's heavy personal, interpersonal and communal impact, there is a clear imperative for developing more efficacious responses to it. The field has been challenged to (a) better identify problematic anger in the presence of PTSD; (b) develop more effective treatments for it and; (c) understand the mechanisms which underlie anger's relationship with PTSD. Several recent important developments in each such area are briefly described.

## Major Research Findings

Dysregulated anger prolongs and exacerbates the impact of PTSD. Importantly, there is evidence that it can be effectively treated. Such outcomes are, however, often less than for other negative affects, like anxiety and depression. Although not yet specifically demonstrated, this may also be the case for anger in the presence of PTSD and the field has been challenged to better identify anger in PTSD and understand its nature and underlying mechanisms, so that better treatments of them are attained.

A significant problem is that the overall modal number of sessions attended by those in treatment for dysfunctional anger is reported to be eight. That session quantum is understood as manifestly inadequate for the delivery of effective treatment and it has been argued that the first challenge in anger treatment generally is to influence clients to continue to attend for treatment.

There are, importantly, evidence-supported treatment components that, if included in a clinician's approach to treating dysregulation, are likely to enhance client motivation to actively participate in treatment. This will first be enhanced by the clinician expertly addressing not only the general relationship of anger with PTSD, but also the differential impact of trauma type on anger in PTSD. Thus, it is important to competently convey to the full range of PTSD sufferers (including victims of child and adult sexual assault, survivors of torture, those occupationally at risk for PTSD and work-place and road-traffic accident survivors) that anger is a key problem that must be addressed to obtain relief from PTSD. Combining what is known about this anger-stressor relationship with an understanding of the importance of predisposing psychological characteristics and behavioural tendencies to anger, via a stress diathesis model of psychopathology, is also critically important here.

Second, the description and application of theoretically well supported treatment rationales — especially, those which emphasise the importance of learning, contextual, emotion regulation, associationist networking and multi-component propositions to dysregulated anger — will, similarly, be important. Doing so provides clinicians and clients with a framework to guide the development of increased anger regulation skills. Underpinning such explanatory theories by the use of intervention models which account for the cognitive mechanisms involved will also be critical here.

Third, the use of a structured and sequential approach to treatment with maximal face validity in treatment is fundamental to the development of treatment efficacy and client commitment to it. Clients with anger dysregulation problems often fear the possibility that they will be incapable of controlling anger and do harm to others, including loved ones. Structured approaches, up to and including, manualised treatment packages can assist in developing and maintaining a sense of order and control within and outside treatment settings.

## Clinical Implications

In the context of this knowledge, the research conducted by the authors demonstrates the use of metrics to gauge anger severity and change is critically important to treatment efficacy and, thereby, client commitment to treatment. This, as the authors have shown, need not be onerous.

The large and clinically meaningful outcomes of the small, uncontrolled 12 session pilot study of a self-instruction training centred manualised individualised treatment for anger in the context of PTSD and the research conducted by the first two authors demonstrating the substantial efficacy of a ten session group treatment program, provide clinically impressive evidence of the benefits of structure in treatment delivery systems. While effective treatment of anger can require more than brief treatment, research by the authors nevertheless shows that focused, brief treatment models can be effectively delivered for both individuals and groups.

The novel and innovative research by the first two authors highlights the importance of imagery in anger in PTSD and imagery's differential interrelationship with thought in angry rumination in different PTSD populations. It points to the need to not only address thought-based cognitions, but also imagery in anger in PTSD, especially where they meet in key phenomena like angry rumination. Treatment that seeks to address uncontrolled imagery associated with anger on account of the specific content of traumatic memories and the recursive nature of those images and measure progress in treatment will be of inherent value to clients.

**Future Directions**

The research described demonstrates that it is possible to (a) quickly and effectively assess for the presence of and changes in problematic anger in a range of populations, including students, survivors of natural disasters (the 2009 Victorian mega bushfire) and different military populations; (b) deliver brief, yet highly effective treatments to military personnel and veterans via manualised individual and group treatments; and

(c) obtain meaningful benefits in treatment outcome in anger in PTSD by exploring not only the impact of thought based cognitions, but also the role of the imagery that may lie at the heart of angry affect and behaviour in PTSD. The challenge from here for researchers and clinicians interested in extending such outcomes is to apply these approaches to other populations. There is evidence that a focus on the operationalisation of measures of imagery and thresholds of imagery dyscontrol may particularly benefit the conceptualisation, measurement and treatment of anger in PTSD.

## Further Readings

Forbes, D., Alkemade, N., Mitchell, D., Elhai, J.D., McHugh, T., Bates, G. ... & Lewis, V. (2014). Utility of the dimensions of anger reactions-5 (DAR-5) scale as a brief anger measure. *Depression and Anxiety, 31*, 166–173.

Forbes, D., McHugh, T., & Chemtob, C. (2013). Regulating anger in combat-related stress disorder. In E. Fernandez (Ed.), *Treatments for anger in specific populations: Theory, application and outcome* (pp. 52–73). New York, NY: Oxford University Press.

McHugh, T., Bates, G., Forbes, D., Hopwood, M., & Creamer, M. (2012). Anger in PTSD: Is there a need for a concept of PTSD-related posttraumatic anger? *Clinical Psychology Review, 32*, 93–104.

Chapter 18

# Adapting CBT for posttraumatic stress disorder and prolonged grief disorder for complex populations and settings

Katie S. Dawson, Fiona Maccallum, Lucy Kenny, and Richard A. Bryant

## Overview

Cognitive-behaviour therapy (CBT) has long been the treatment of choice for posttraumatic stress disorder (PTSD). Central to trauma-focused CBT are the following elements: (a) reframing maladaptive trauma appraisals identified to maintain distress (cognitive therapy); (b) verbal processing of the trauma memory (prolonged exposure); and (c) behavioural modification aimed to help an individual gradually confront trauma-related stimuli (in vivo exposure). However, the application of CBT across various complex presentations presents challenges for the clinician. This chapter considers how CBT can be adapted for clients with prolonged grief disorder (PGD); to address the complex interplay of PTSD and comorbid difficulties many police officers experience; and finally, to meet global mental health needs in low- and middle-income countries (LMICs) where mental health professionals are scarce.

## Major Findings

Disabling reactions to bereavement have received considerable attention in recent years. DSM-5 introduced persistent and complex bereavement disorder as a condition for further study and the upcoming ICD-11 has proposed a new diagnosis termed prolonged grief disorder. Grief-CBT, comprising education, cognitive restructuring, exposure to loss memories, in vivo exposure, communication with the deceased, and goal setting has been developed to treat PGD. Initial studies highlight the efficacy of this approach. However, a significant number of people fail to respond and there are ongoing questions about the necessary components of treatment. A key debate revolves around the appropriateness of exposure, a strategy typically used to target anxiety-related avoidance. PGD, however, is not necessarily characterised by avoidance; instead yearning and proximity-seeking are prominent. To test the efficacy of exposure, individuals participating in group grief-CBT were randomly assigned to receive additional supportive counselling or exposure therapy for memories of the death. Those who received exposure therapy showed greater symptom improvement over the short and longer term. Characteristics of the loss did not impact outcomes.

Similarly, CBT has been proven to be effective in treating PTSD in civilian populations; however, the evidence is more limited for populations exposed to trauma in the workplace. Police officers are exposed to multiple traumatic events in the course of their duties and operate in a culture that often exacerbates stress and encourages coping strategies, such as avoidance and suppression. Accordingly, rates of PTSD are elevated in this population. However, PTSD is often accompanied by comorbid difficulties which can impact on treatment engagement and outcome. These include limited emotional awareness, profound emotional numbing or avoidance, challenges related to their sense of identity, poorly managed anger, and a general lack of trust in mental health professionals, who are often viewed as not understanding the culture and unique demands of their work. The complex interplay of these themes in presentation offer unique challenges to clinicians that are critical to navigate appropriately when assessing and treating police officers.

From a global perspective, we know trauma and loss do not discriminate and mental illness remains a significant burden of disease. However, few evidence-based therapies are available in LMICs, where the majority of the global population resides. The most notable barrier to accessing treatments is the grossly insufficient number of mental health professionals in these settings. Adapting CBT to promote a 'task-shifting' approach (training available and affordable lay-providers only in the intervention) provides a sustainable response to addressing the treatment gap. Problem Management Plus is an example of such an intervention. It is a brief, low-intensity intervention, emphasising behavioural components to address the constellation of mental health symptoms individuals in LMICs experience. It is currently being trialled in several trauma-exposed settings with promising results.

### Clinical Implications

While CBT-based interventions show promise in treating PDG, PTSD in police officers and when delivered in LMICs, this chapter highlights the idiosyncratic features that accompany these populations one needs to be mindful of and adapt treatments accordingly. For instance, in the case of PGD we hypothesise that facilitating emotional responses to the death may promote greater changes in appraisals regarding the loss, which are associated with symptom reduction. Treatments for PGD should therefore include strategies that promote emotional processing of the loss.

When working with police officers, it is recommended that clinicians discriminate between symptoms of re-experiencing that provoke anxiety as opposed to depressive rumination, as well as assessing comorbid issues such as suppression, anger, identity and trust. Accordingly, a modified CBT protocol for treating PTSD in this population requires an integration of standard techniques with additional sessions targeting these themes in a way that is palatable for police officers.

Finally, in LMICs we suggest that adaptation of CBT interventions emphasise three components believed to be critical in supporting scale-up while preserving treatment effectiveness: (a) brevity — to reduce treatment attrition and improve cost-effectiveness, (b) low-intensity — simplified strategies to enhance learning by intervention deliverers and clients over a short period of time; and (c) cultural adaptation — to ensure acceptability and appropriateness for the local context.

## Future Directions

This chapter presents some preliminary research into the adaptation of CBT for complex presentations (PGD and PTSD in police officers) and settings (humanitarian settings where task-shifting is necessary). Despite a long history of interest in clinical presentations among these populations, it is only recently that rigorous empirical methods have been applied. As we better understand key mechanisms underlying PGD and police-related PTSD, CBT will become more tailored to core maintaining factors. Further research testing the effectiveness of adapted-CBT delivered by lay-providers is required if we want to make concerted efforts to reduce the treatment gap in LMICs.

## Further Reading

Bryant, R.A., Kenny, L., Joscelyne, A., Rawson, N., Maccallum, F., Cahill, C., ... Nickerson, A. (2014). Treating prolonged grief disorder: A randomized controlled trial. *JAMA Psychiatry, 71*, 1332–1339.

Haugen, P.T., Evces, M. & Weiss, D.S. (2012). Treating posttraumatic stress disorder in first responders: A systematic review. *Clinical Psychology Review, 32*, 370–380.

Dawson, K.S., Bryant, R.A., Harper, M., Tay, A.K., Rahman, A., Schafer, A. & van Ommeren, M. (2015). Problem Management Plus (PM+): A WHO transdiagnostic psychological intervention for common mental health problems. *World Psychiatry, 14*, 354–357.

Section 5

Obesity and Eating Disorders

Chapter 19

# Novel interventions for eating disorders and other transdiagnostic outcomes

Mia Pellizzer and Tracey Wade

## Overview

Eating disorders are mental illnesses that significantly impair psychosocial and physical functioning. Given that around 13% of females will have had an eating disorder by age 20, and that individuals with eating disorders utilise health services more than any other form of mental illness, there is a strong need for accessible and efficacious treatments. Cognitive behaviour therapy — enhanced (CBT-E), the current gold standard treatment for eating disorders for people aged 16 years and over, has been found to help approximately 50% of clients recover. Therefore improvements to therapy are required in order to better help the remaining 50% of clients. A focus on perfectionism, mindfulness, and cognitive bias are candidates for possible augmentations to cognitive-behaviour therapy (CBT) approaches. Each has shown promise in reducing eating disorder symptoms in addition to improving anxiety, depression, and wellbeing. Future research is needed to conduct dismantling studies that directly compare CBT-E with each possible augmentation to determine whether significant benefit is conferred for certain subgroups.

## Major Findings

To date, CBT-E has been the most evaluated treatment for eating disorders. A randomised controlled trial (RCT) comparing CBT-E to a wait list control found approximately 50% of participants had disordered eating less than one standard deviation above the community mean by end of treatment and follow up. Other published evaluations have found comparable results. Comparisons between a broad form of CBT-E that includes modules for mood intolerance, clinical perfectionism, low self-esteem, and interpersonal difficulties to a focused form of CBT-E (treating eating disorder cognitions and behaviours only) found no statistically significant differences between the two forms. However, 60% of participants in the broad CBT-E group who had complex psychopathology were found to have a good treatment response compared to 40% who received the focused form. This finding suggests that further research regarding the augmentation of CBT-E may prove informative, especially where the augmentation has the ability to work transdiagnostically on complex psychopathology.

Our research has investigated the degree to which manipulating levels of perfectionism, mindfulness, and cognitive bias can have an impact on disordered eating. Clinical perfectionism has been linked with both causing and maintaining eating disorders, in addition to anxiety and depression, providing a transdiagnostic treatment target. Treatment of perfectionism without a focus on disorder-specific symptoms has been found to decrease eating disorder symptoms, depression and anxiety.

Mindfulness-based interventions (MBI) are another trans-diagnostic treatment approach that has been shown to improve general wellbeing, stress and depression, in addition to body dissatisfaction and binge eating. A randomised controlled trial (RCT) compared a mindfulness-based prevention program to a dissonance-based program and a control condition in a sample of adolescent girls. While there were no statistically significant differences between the two active programs, when facilitated by an expert, only the mindfulness condition showed significant improvements in weight and shape concern, dietary restraint, thin-ideal internalisation, eating disorder symptoms and psychosocial impairment compared to the control condition. The findings demonstrate promise in applying mindfulness to eating disorder treatment.

A third transdiagnostic contender for treatment augmentation is cognitive bias modification (CBM). Body dissatisfaction and negative affect are both risk factors for eating disorders that are driven in part by attentional and interpretive biases for appearance and self-worth related information. CBM may be applied to retrain such biases, including interpretation biases related to self, and as such CBM may provide a promising avenue for eating disorder treatment to explore.

### Clinical Implications

Evaluation of augmentation of CBT for eating disorders for those patients with complex psychopathology is an important area of enquiry. In particular, consideration of manipulating perfectionism, mindfulness, and cognitive biases would appear to be potentially useful avenues of enquiry to explore. Such transdiagnostic approaches offer an efficient way to target multiple disorders and difficulties simultaneously including depression, anxiety, self-esteem, and general wellbeing.

## Future Directions

While preliminary evidence of augmentation of CBT may produce greater reductions in eating disorder symptoms for those with complex psychopathology, more definitive research is required. Dismantling studies that compare CBT-E with augmented forms of CBT-E are required to evaluate whether such adjuncts are capable of improving treatment outcomes and remission rates.

## Further Readings

Atkinson, M.J., & Wade, T.D. (2015). Mindfulness-based prevention for eating disorders: A school-based cluster randomized controlled study. *International Journal of Eating Disorders, 48*(7), 1024–1037. doi:10.1002/eat.22416

Egan, S., Wade, T.D., Shafran, R., & Antony, M. (2014). *Cognitive-behavioural treatment of perfectionism.* New York, NY: Guilford.

Fairburn, C.G., Cooper, Z., Doll, H.A., O'Connor, M., Bohn, K., Hawker, D.M., … Palmer, R.L. (2009). Transdiagnostic cognitive-behavioral therapy for patients with eating disorders: A two-site trial with 60-week follow-up. *The American Journal of Psychiatry, 166*(3), 311–319. doi:10.1176/appi.ajp.2008.08040608

Chapter 20

# Automatic processes in eating behaviour: Understanding and overcoming food cue-reactivity

Leentje Vervoort, Karolien Van den Akker, Ghislaine Schyns, Naomi Kakoschke, Eva Kemps, and Caroline Braet

## Overview

People not only eat because they are hungry; food intake is often triggered by food cues in the environment. For example, the smell of Belgian waffles might tempt you to buy and eat one on a day out shopping with friends, even when you have only just finished lunch. In the present obesogenic environment, food cue-reactivity is indeed an important determinant of eating behaviour, often overriding homeostatic signals of satiety. The method of choice in the experimental study of cue-reactivity is the classical conditioning paradigm, and there is ample evidence for the applicability of the appetitive conditioning paradigm as a model for cue-elicited cravings and eating behaviour. Cue-elicited eating seems to be automatic and beyond conscious control, thereby increasing the risk of overeating and related weight problems. Research in the food domain has focused on two automatic cognitive processes, namely attentional bias and approach bias, which have been demonstrated to contribute to eating behaviour.

## Major Findings

Such automatic processes associated with food cue-reactivity and described in cognitive-motivational models have been found to be important determinants of maladaptive eating behaviour.

## Clinical Implications

Targeting these automatic processes may be a useful cognitive intervention aimed at improving eating behaviours. Approach bias modification has been shown to successfully re-train and modify the approach bias toward unhealthy food cues. In addition, the effects of such training on implicit preferences for unhealthy food can be further enhanced by inhibitory control training. As for attentional bias modification, evidence shows that training overweight and obese individuals to avoid unhealthy food cues over multiple sessions effectively reduces the attentional bias for such food cues, and encouragingly, these training effects can be sustained over some time, thereby showing near and far transfer effects with, among others, effects on weight loss.

Theories of learning and behaviour neatly describe how cues elicit behaviour. Several studies indeed show that repeated pairings of an initially neutral stimulus with food intake leads to increased cravings when confronted with the intake-associated cue. Theories of learning and behaviour therefore provide valuable insights on the determinants of eating behaviour and overweight. However, when they propose a single determining factor, they are at risk of being overly simplistic. Contemporary learning theories stress that the determining role of any given factor (i.e., conditioning) can only be understood when additional factors, like personality traits, are taken into account. Impulsivity, for example, has been found to affect acquisition and extinction of appetitive responses. Another personality trait that is very relevant for eating behaviour, is Reward Sensitivity. Reward Sensitivity is a psychobiological personality trait, related to activity in the reward regions in the brain and referring to an individual's ability to experience pleasure or reward on exposure to appetitive stimuli (i.e., palatable foods). If an individual reacts more strongly to an appetitive stimulus than others, it might be assumed that this moderates conditioning processes. Conditioning might also be influenced by other individual characteristics. Several studies show indeed that overweight individuals show differential acquisition and extinction patterns compared with normal-weight individuals, which could have consequences for weight-loss interventions.

While traditional weight-loss interventions generally seem ineffective to reduce overeating and weight on the long-term, learning theory predicts that directly targeting learned associations between food cues and intake might lead to more sustainable reductions in overeating and weight. This is the goal of food cue-exposure therapy, during which overweight and/or eating disordered individuals are repeatedly exposed to food-associated cues (e.g., the sight and smell of palatable food), while intake is not allowed. Recent data indicate that cue-exposure therapy indeed reduces overeating, weight and eating psychopathology in overweight individuals. Automatic food cue-reactivity is an important factor in understanding eating behaviour and tackling weight problems. The novel approach of intervening with food cue-reactivity, both from a cognitive-motivational and a cognitive behavioural point of view, is particularly relevant within the context of the present obesogenic environment with its abundance of food-cue-triggers, widespread unhealthy eating habits in both young-sters and adults, and the alarming obesity rates worldwide.

## Future Directions

There is growing evidence for the efficacy of interventions tar-geting automatic food cue-reactivity. Under ideal research circumstances, such interventions produce beneficial effects. Future research should study the conditions in which these effects might generalise to other contexts and establish evidence for their effectiveness in real world settings. However, it should be noted that targeting food cue-reactivity in isolation would not produce sustainable weight loss. Importantly, treatment of obesity requires a multidisciplinary life-style approach that focuses not only on diet and eating behaviour, but also on physical activity. Therefore, future research should explore how novel food-cue reactivity tech-niques can be integrated into existing evidence-based interventions to increase their efficacy.

## Further Reading

van den Akker, K., Havermans, R.C., Bouton, M.E., Jansen, A. (2014). How partial reinforcement of food cues affects the extinction and reacquisition of affective responses: A new model for dieting success? *Appetite, 81*, 242–252.

Kemps, E., & Tiggemann, M. (2015). Approach bias for food cues in obese individuals. *Psychology & Health, 30*, 370–380.

Kakoschke, N., Kemps, E., & Tiggemann, M. (2015). Combined effects of cognitive bias for food cues and poor inhibitory control on unhealthy food intake. *Appetite, 87*, 358–364.

Chapter 21

# Food: Treat or threat or treatment? Reward and punishment in eating behaviour and interventions to change them

Leentje Vervoort, Laura Vandeweghe, Karolien Van den Akker, Nienke Jonker, Caroline Braet, and Eva Kemps

## Overview

The reinforcing value of food is a strong determinant of food intake, often overriding homeostatic signals of deprivation and satiety. For most people, food is a treat (reward), however, for some (e.g., people with eating disorders), it can be a threat (punishment). Individual differences in reward and punishment processing (sensitivity to reward and punishment) are related to food reinforcement. Insight on the reinforcing characteristics of food might be of crucial interest for interventions (treatment) aiming to improve eating behaviour and diet quality.

## Major Findings

People not only eat because they are food deprived, but also because eating gives them pleasure. Eating because of food deprivation is aimed at restoring energy balance and can be referred to as homeostatic hunger. Hedonic eating, however, is driven by the pleasure that is associated with eating. Consistent with this intrinsic rewarding character of food, most people enjoy eating. However, the foods from which people derive the most pleasure, and ones that are abundantly available in the present obesogenic environment, are those that tend to be the most calorically dense. High energy, less healthy foods are considered to be more rewarding than low energy, healthier foods. Nonetheless, the reward value of healthy food can be increased, for example through associative conditioning procedures.

Despite the fact that food is a primary reinforcer, not all individuals are equally sensitive to the rewarding aspects of food. The reward value of food is determined, among others, by an individual's weight status (with increased food reward observed in obese people), gender (with increased food reward seen in boys), and hunger (with increased food reward under food deprivation). The influence of the reward value of food might be particularly relevant for individuals with high dispositional sensitivity to reward. Sensitivity to reward is a psychobiological personality trait, related to activity in the reward regions of the brain, and refers to an individual's ability to experience pleasure or reward in response to exposure to appetitive stimuli (i.e., palatable foods). This personality trait is particularly important in the understanding of eating behaviour. For example, consumption of fast food, snacks and sugar sweetened beverages is higher in individuals with a higher sensitivity to reward. Furthermore, studies have shown that the acquisition of conditioned responses to food cues and their extinction might be influenced by sensitivity to reward and other aspects of impulsivity.

Despite the strong motivational character of food, food may not necessarily be rewarding for all individuals. For example, neophobic children are afraid of novel foods, and for people with high dispositional sensitivity to punishment, the short term reinforcing effect of food might be considered a problem. Sensitivity to punishment is a psychobiological personality trait, related to activity in the septohippocampal regions of the brain, and refers to an individual's susceptibility to aversive stimuli. This personality trait can be associated with the fear of becoming overweight and obese, and might result in the motivation to lose weight by dieting. For individuals who are highly responsive to both punishment and reward, this may result in a vulnerability for unsuccessful dieting behaviour. This might be especially the case for individuals with low executive control since they are less able to direct thoughts and actions towards obtaining their dieting goals.

## Clinical Implications

Interventions aimed at improving eating behaviour and promoting weight loss often use reward strategies, based on insights from theories of learning and behaviour. For example, reward-based parent management training (cognitive-behaviour therapy [CBT]) for weight reduction in overweight children, can lead to sustained weight loss and positive changes in the eating behaviour of children and families. However, the effect of such treatments might be dependent on an individual's sensitivity to reward. It is very likely that treatments or strategies in which rewards are used are more effective for children high in reward sensitivity. The critical aspect of strategies to improve children's liking and consumption of food items is familiarising children with the taste of the food item by bringing the food item into contact with the taste buds. A high reward sensitive child might be more eager to taste if she/he knows she/he will be rewarded for tasting. As a consequence the learning process might be facilitated in high reward sensitive children. To conclude, food can act as a reward (treat) or a punishment (threat), depending on individual characteristics like weight status and dispositional sensitivity to reward or punishment. The reinforcing value of food and sensitivity to reward and punishment can be considered strong determinants of both normal and disordered eating behaviour. Taking into consideration the reward value of food and reward and punishment sensitivity when developing interventions to improve enhance eating behaviour is a promising way to increase the effectiveness of such efforts.

## Future Directions

Future research should consider reward and punishment, and their interactions, at those three levels (reinforcing value of food, individual differences and treatment) in order to fully understand their implications for both normal and disordered eating behaviour. Furthermore, consistent with a bio-psychosocial view, the concepts should be studied in relation to other known determinants of eating behaviour (e.g., individual factors, like socioeconomic status (SES) and pubertal state; social factors, like peer and family influences; characteristics of the physical environment, like healthy food availability).

## Further Reading

Davis, C., Strachan, S., & Berkson, M. (2004). Sensitivity to reward. Implications for overeating and overweight. *Appetite, 42*, 131–138.

De Cock, N., Van Lippevelde, W., Vervoort, L., Vangeel, J., Maes, L., Eggermont, S., ... Van Camp, J. (in press). Sensitivity to reward is associated with snack and sugar sweetened beverage consumption in adolescents. *European Journal of Nutrition.*

van den Akker, K., Havermans, R.C., Bouton, M.E., Jansen, A. (2014). How partial reinforcement of food cues affects the extinction and reacquisition of affective responses: A new model for dieting success? *Appetite, 81,* 242–252.

Chapter 22

# Child and adolescent Obesity: Is cognitive-behaviour therapy part of our solution?

Gerri Minshall and Caroline Braet

## Overview

Paediatric obesity is a massive problem confronting researchers, clinicians and citizens. General prevalence rates are stabilising but extreme child/adolescent obesity is increasing and becoming more socioeconomically patterned. The problem is multi-factorial with a variety of powerful 'upstream drivers'. When faced with a problem so big and complex, an effective treatment obviously involves multiple components but they all have in common that life-long lifestyle behavioural changes are needed. Based on scientific evidence, cognitive-behaviour therapy (CBT), focusing on effective behavioural change, becomes our 'scaffold' or guiding approach whatever is the predominant form of treatment in a given country. Forms of treatments enacted across the world include — parenting education (conceptualised in the obesity literature as parents as 'agents of change') bariatric surgery for adolescents, residential (camps and boarding schools) or outpatient groups/appointments. Research into individual psychological mechanisms feeds back into ensuring CBT becomes more targeted. Our solution to this problem will need to be multi-faceted and without a doubt CBT is needed to help extremely obese youth lose weight.

## Major Findings

One in five (20%) children between 2 and 17 years old are overweight; about 7% of them are obese. While prevalence levels of paediatric obesity are stabilising, social disparity is increasing — levels are declining in high SES youth and increasing in lower SES groups. Also of note — extreme obesity — defined as body mass indexes (BMIs) over 35, is reaching high levels in some population subgroups. So some of our most vulnerable youth are also becoming heavier. It is not unusual for specialised services such as mental health, disability or rehabilitation (not only obesity services) to encounter, for example, a young teen weighing around 120 kg.

So, an important characteristic of extreme obesity is that some key maintaining factors are external to the individual and are powerful societal forces. The main drivers are the obesogenic food environment, the built environment, and the psycho-social environment. These constructs in turn include neighbourhood design, advertising, food pricing and the normality of recreational screen use. Put in cognitive-behavioural terms all of the contingencies in modern society reward obesogenic behaviours whereas the opposite, family-wide healthy lifestyle behaviours tend to be effortful, time consuming and more expensive.

Family-based behavioural lifestyle treatment is the current treatment of choice for pediatric obesity and recommended in the newest World Health Organization (WHO) report on ending childhood obesity. The behavioural lifestyle intervention offered as multidisciplinary obesity treatment involves a combination of diet, physical activity, , reducing screen time and behavioural treatment (CBT), including parental involvement. These variables can be addressed by (1) a multidisciplinary outpatient setting where groups may be offered; (2) an immersion/residential treatment such a boarding school or camp and; (3) bariatric surgery (for adolescents).

Multidisciplinary treatment services are advocated because obese children and adolescents have been found to suffer increased levels of medical, psycho-social and psychological comorbidities than their healthy weight (or even over weight range) peers. Parents have also been found to be more distressed and suffer higher rates of anxiety and depression. Researchers are building a useful knowledge base of how obese youth are different in terms of constructs such as (1) attachment style; (2) degree of emotional eating; (3) degree of restraint/impulsive eating and; (4) executive functioning abilities.

According to the Cochrane Review of 2009 outpatient treatment can be effective but it needs to be intensive enough and involve long term follow up. However, questions remain. Lifestyle treatments tend not to help children/adolescents lose large amounts of weight or change their BMI z-score. An obesity treatment is effortful and involves adherence, multiple behaviour changes and building new skills in the context of an individual who may be biologically and psychologically disposed to gain weight and who probably lives in an environment not supportive of a healthy lifestyle. It should be noted that while alternatives are attractive, they do have pitfalls as well. A randomised controlled trial (RCT) has been conducted on obese adolescents comparing gastric banding to a lifestyle modification program. At two-year follow-up the gastric banding group had lost and average of 34.6 kg while the lifestyle intervention group around 3 kg. However, one of the problems in adolescence is that they are less adherent than adults with regard to postoperative care, whereby complications were observed in 70% of the adolescents.

To conclude, although challenging, CBT can build a unified treatment strategy for these immense challenges.

## Clinical Implications

We need a clear rationale, focusing on weight control through CBT techniques so that families were not disappointed about the moderate weight loss. Interestingly, a moderate reduction of 0.6 BMI (standard deviation score [SDS], the most crucial weight index) due to a behavioural lifestyle treatment program, can reduce the medical comorbidities significantly. Even more importantly, when a treatment success of > 0.5 BMI (SDS) reduction can be maintained, this is seen as clinically relevant.

As is easily imagined, when many components of a family's lifestyle needs to be changed, we need a methodology which can harness and track a large amount of behavioural detail. It is essential to assess and address particular barriers to weight loss which can include specific parental behaviours such as no time to prepare food, or child, adolescent or parent beliefs such as 'I don't think I'm obese' or 'They will grow out of it'. There almost always are long standing, family ways of operating such as many hours of screen time and/or a later bedtime which maintain obesity. Families may also not have the skills to enact positive, healthy lifestyle strategies such as ensuring their adolescent eats breakfast or sharing a family meal at a table with no screens. A good example of treatment targeting this skills deficit is the service at The Children's Hospital at Westmead which focuses on parental monitoring skills such as keeping track of your child's weight.

Specific CBT techniques which have been researched and found to be useful in weight loss treatments are goal setting, monitoring and stimulus control. Interestingly these key strategies can apply to all of the lifestyle domains of (1) diet, (2) physical activity, and (3) reducing sedentary behaviour (screen time).

Almost every cognitive-behavioural technique could be applied to weight loss and quality programs tend to include a lot of behavioural techniques. Good examples here are The Princess Margaret Hospital in Perth, which conducts an adolescent group which teaches cognitive and problem solving skills such as dealing with weight discrimination and body image concerns. Also, the Zeepreventorium in De Haan, Belgium is a residential setting where youngsters are learning CBT techniques, taught how to cook and prepare healthy meals and track their food intake and physical activity on home visits.

## Future Directions

Future research needs to address predictors of weight loss success for children/adolescents or families and predictors of weight loss success for adolescents undertaking bariatric surgery. We are starting to build a knowledge foundation of how obese children/adolescents are different in terms of their attachment, family functioning, restraint/impulsivity/style of eating but now we need to know if addressing these variables in treatment leads to a better weight loss result. We do not really know if the effective components of adult weight loss programs are as useful when treating the obese paediatric clientele. How can parents enact so many changes needed in an obesogenic modern world and what sort of support do they prefer?

All of these questions start to answer what are the essential skills and content needed for a cognitive-behavioural weight loss syllabus.

## Further Reading

Fredrick, C.B., Snelman, K., & Putnam, R.D. (2014). Increasing socioeconomic disparities in adolescent obesity. *PNAS, 111*(4), 1338–1342.

World Health Organization. (2016). *Report of the Commission on Ending Childhood Obesity*. Geneva, Switzerland: Author.

Section 6

Depression and Bipolar Disorders

Chapter 23

# Cognitive processes: The role of rumination in depression and transdiagnostically

Michelle L. Moulds, Katie Chung, Ann Martin, and Suraj Samtani

## Overview

Depression is characterised by disturbances in an array of cognitive processes. Among such disturbances are depressed individuals' tendency to engage in maladaptive repetitive thinking in the form of depressive rumination. Our focus here is on understanding the role of rumination in depression, as well as the nature and role of repetitive thinking across psychological disorders. Our hope is that our work will meet our goal of increasing our understanding of the interplay between cognitive processes and the processing of both positive and negative material, with a view to translating the outcomes in order to develop novel interventions for managing depressive conditions.

## Major Findings

Rumination refers to persistent, repetitive thinking about one's self, one's emotions, as well as experiences and events that have occurred in the past. The late Professor Susan Hoeksema's seminal theoretical work in the early 1990s was the catalyst for the now expansive literature on the topic of depressive rumination, defined as responding to sad mood with thoughts that focus on depressive symptoms and their causes, meanings and consequences. There is much evidence that individuals who engage in depressive rumination when they are in a sad mood are more likely to become clinically depressed, and further, to stay depressed for longer. When rumination is induced in the laboratory, it contributes to the persistence of a range of depression-related deficits, such as poor problem-solving and the retrieval of overgeneral memories. More recent investigations have shown that it is not simply that engaging in rumination per se is problematic for depressed individuals. Rather, it is rumination that is abstract/evaluative (e.g., *why can't I feel better? why can't I cope with my problems as well as everyone else can?*) that has adverse effects. Alternatively, prompting depressed individuals to adopt a concrete style of repetitive thinking (e.g., *what can I do to help myself to begin to feel better? what steps can I take to solve my problems?*) leads to beneficial outcomes.

Studies that investigate whether the cognitive processes such as rumination which play a role in depression are also present in individuals with a history of depression are critical in order to clarify whether such processes are trait-like and potentially confer vulnerability to depression, or whether they persist beyond the resolution of a depressive episode, and thus may be conceptualised as a 'scar' of having experienced the disorder. There is empirical evidence that individuals who engage in rumination premorbidly (i.e., before they are ever diagnosed with depression) have a greater likelihood of developing depression symptoms following a stressor. In addition, there is evidence that individuals who have recovered from depression continue to engage in rumination — at comparable levels to currently depressed individuals — even when their symptoms have remitted.

What is not well understood is whether individuals with a more chronic history of depression (i.e., individuals who have experienced multiple episodes of depression) engage in rumination more frequently and more readily when they experience sad mood, and as such, whether rumination may play a role in depressive relapse. The number of previous depressive episodes that an individual has experienced is a robust predictor of depression recurrence: the greater the number of previous episodes, the higher the risk of recurrence. Although preliminary, our findings to date suggest that there are no differences between formerly depressed individuals who have experienced only one previous depressive episode and those who have a more chronic history (two, three or more episodes) in the extent to which they engage in rumination in response to sad mood.

Given the well-established role of rumination in depression, most investigations of the nature and consequences of this type of thinking have been conducted in the depression literature. However, the tendency to engage in repetitive thought is not a clinical characteristic of depressed individuals only: socially anxious individuals report repetitive thinking in anticipation of and following social events, individuals diagnosed with posttraumatic stress disorder (PTSD) describe dwelling on the memory of their trauma, and individuals with generalised anxiety disorder report repetitive worries about anticipated future events. Empirical evidence has accrued that confirms the role of ruminative thinking across clinical disorders. Until recently, most self-report measures that assess rumination have been disorder-specific; that is, they have indexed rumination in the context of a particular clinical presentation (e.g., rumination about sad mood in depression). Such measures significantly limit clinicians' ability to meaningfully assess rumination across disorders, or across comorbid conditions. In recent years, important developments have been made in the measurement of rumination, insomuch as a number of instruments have been published which enable clinicians and researchers to assess repetitive thinking transdiagnostically (i.e., irrespective of the disorder with which an individual is diagnosed, and irrespective of the presence and nature of any comorbid diagnoses).

## Clinical Implications

Our findings converge on some recommendations for assessment and treatment. Specifically, the clinical assessment of depressed individuals, as well as those with a history of depression, should include detailed questioning about and assessment of the content, nature and impact of rumination. Information gained from such an assessment should be incorporated into a client's case formulation and guide decisions about the key maintaining factors to be addressed in the intervention.

## Future Directions

The literature described earlier raises some timely and exciting challenges for theory and practice in this area. First, in order to make advances, clinical researchers need to continue to develop and validate self-report instruments that index rumination. Such measures should not be limited to a particular disorder, but rather, measure ruminative thinking regardless of clinical presentation. In addition, given that abstract thinking has been isolated as the core maladaptive feature of rumination, there is a pressing need to develop measures that distinguish abstract from concrete rumination.

Second, the continued development and evaluation of interventions that aim to reduce rumination should be a research priority, with the goals of both effectively treating depression and reducing rates of relapse. Third, in light of the prevalence of rumination across disorders, experimental work is needed for us to fully understand the cognitive underpinnings of repetitive thinking transdiagnostically, which will forge the way for refinements in theory and enable clinical innovation.

## Further Readings

McEvoy, P.M., Mahoney, A., & Moulds, M.L. (2010). Are worry, rumination, and post-event processing one and the same? Development of the Repetitive Thinking Questionnaire. *Journal of Anxiety Disorders, 24,* 509–519.

Watkins, E. (2008). Constructive and unconstructive repetitive thought. *Psychological Bulletin, 134,* 163–206.

Werner-Seidler, A., & Moulds, M.L. (2014). Recalling positive self-defining memories in depression: The impact of processing mode. *Memory, 22,* 525–535.

Chapter 24

# New psychosocial approaches to bipolar disorder

Thilo Deckersbach, Weilynn C. Chang, Amy T. Peters, Jonathan P. Stange, Alexandra K. Gold, Casey M. Hearing, Louisa G. Sylvia, Michael Berk, Pedro Vieira da Silva Magalhaes, Darin Doughert,y and Andrew A. Nierenberg

## Overview

Bipolar disorder (BD) is characterised by episodes of mania and also depression. It affects approximately 2.6% of American adults. Through the course of their illness, bipolar patients tend to progressively experience worse functioning and quality of life, both of which are factors associated with higher rates of suicide and greater negative impacts on families and communities. Thus, it is important to highlight existing treatments, as well as where further advancements may be needed. The first line of treatment for individuals with BD is pharmacotherapy. However, pharmacotherapy tends to fail to bring any bipolar patients to sustained symptomatic and functional remission. Therefore, the efficacy of evidence-based psychosocial interventions as an adjunctive form of treatment has been explored. Although such interventions have demonstrated benefits for these patients in terms of relapse prevention, medication adherence, shortening time spent in a depressed episode, and improving supportive relationships, overall functioning and quality of life often remain impaired for these patients. In order to continue to advance treatment options for these patients, the purpose of this chapter is to discuss various adjunctive psychosocial interventions, as well as web based initiatives that may have promise for improving symptoms and functioning.

## Major Findings

Thirty to forty per cent of bipolar patients have significant cognitive impairments. This involves impairments in attention, memory and executive functioning (planning and problem solving). In the domain of memory, patients with BD (even when not manic or depressed) have difficulties learning/establishing new memories. This could interfere with their ability to form or retain new memories that are presumably needed to benefit from psychotherapy. In a recent study Deckersbach and colleagues compared cognitive-behaviour therapy (CBT) for depression with supportive psychotherapy (SP) for depressed patients with bipolar I disorder. Although patients receiving CBT tended to experience relief from depression faster than patients with SP, there was no overall difference in the degree to which both treatments decreased depression. Before the start of treatment, patients completed tests of learning and memory (e.g., the California Verbal Learning Test [CVLT]). Deckersbach and colleagues found that the learning of new words in the CVLT was not predictive for the degree of response to psychotherapy. However, retention of words over a longer delay predicted treatment response. This finding suggests that the degree to which a patient is able to retain new memories (i.e., content retained from a therapy session) over time is critical in predicting how much they are able to benefit from treatment (i.e., CBT or SP). Additionally, individuals who scored lower in tests of cognitive flexibility exhibited slower decrease of depression symptoms.

Access to tailored effective therapies is a major obstacle for bipolar patients not only in the United States (US), but probably world-wide. Therefore, treatment initiatives have been shifted towards developing types of interventions for bipolar patients that are web-based. One such online initiative called iCARE4bipolar was rigorously designed with the help of end-users and experts in the field. This website is aimed at being an easily accessible online resource for family and friends of adults with bipolar disorder, which is especially important given how crucial supportive relationships are for the course of one's illness.

In addition to iCARE4bipolar, another online intervention that exists is MoodSwings 2.0, a platform that includes discussion boards. The role discussion boards may play in improving psychosocial outcomes is still unclear. Gliddon and colleagues from Deakin University are currently investigating whether engagement with discussion boards (quantity of posts/number of visits) would influence outcomes. Preliminary results suggest discussion board engagement may have an effect on mania symptom severity in people with bipolar disorder in the short term (baseline to 3 months follow up). However, it remains unclear if the discussion boards help to reduce mania symptom severity or if those with fewer mania symptoms are more likely to engage with the discussion boards.

Finally, recently, the MoodNetwork (www.moodnetwork.org; funded by the Patient-Centered Outcomes Research Institute) was launched. The MoodNetwork is an online community for individuals with mood disorders. The primary aim of this online initiative is to connect at least 50,000 people with bipolar disorder or depression to conduct comparative effectiveness research on an unprecedented scale. MoodNetwork is the first patient-powered research network for individuals with mood disorders and will serve as a platform for research studies and as a resource where patients can track their symptoms, engage in forums, ask study clinicians questions about mood disorders, and prioritise areas of research. It serves as a forum where patients have input into the design of studies. This allows for the running of large-scale studies, which provides opportunities for patients around the world to participate. It recently launched a mobile sensing study to validate smart phones as a means of tracking patients' behaviours (without them needing to do mood ratings) to predict the recurrence of depression or mania symptoms. Such studies will play an integral role in developing predictive models for early interventions that prevent relapse into depression or mania. Since its launch, MoodNetwork has enrolled 2346 participants. 96.0% of participants report experiencing depression and 80.2% endorse experiencing mania or hypomania.

## Clinical Implications

Findings from these four studies suggest that there is a continued need to advance our knowledge on what types of interventions are the most effective, as well as what factors influence their effectiveness. Understanding that retention may be predictive of psychotherapy outcomes highlights memory enhancement tasks as a useful treatment target. The iCARE4 model could potentially be a cost-effective way to inform, support and up-skill family and friends who have a vital supportive role. Having a greater understanding of the impact discussion boards may have on outcomes in bipolar disorder (i.e., MoodSwings 2.0) will help to inform the development of future self-guided programs. Finally, the MoodNetwork's patient-centric approach allows for participants to offer patient perspectives on which research topics should be prioritised.

## Future Directions

iCARE4bipolar, MoodSwings 2.0 and the MoodNetwork all demonstrate promise in developing patient-centric interventions that may improve outcomes and functioning for individuals with mood disorders. Future research should continue to examine the efficacy of such interventions, and to more closely investigate who benefits most from these treatments.

## Further Readings

Deckersbach, T., Nierenberg, A.A., Kessler, R., Lund, H.G., Ametrano, R.M., Sachs, G., ... Dougherty, D.D. (2010). Cognitive rehabilitation for bipolar disorder: An open trial for employed patients with residual depressive symptoms. *CNS Neuroscience and Therapeutics, 16*, 298–307. NIHMSID: NIHMS149948

Nierenberg, A.A., Sylvia, L.G., Doederlein, A., Edgman-Levitan, S., Muskin, A., Jewell, L., ... R., Deckersbach, T. (2015). Improving the care of patients who have treatment-resistant depression: The promise of the PCORnet MoodNetwork. *Journal of Clinical Psychiatry, 76(4)*. doi 10.4088/JCP.14com09570

Chapter 25

# Predictors and moderators of treatment response for psychotherapy for depression in bipolar disorder

Thilo Deckersbach, Alexandra K. Gold, Amy T. Peters, Jonathan P. Stange, Weilynn C. Chang, Louisa G. Sylvia, Michael Berk, Pedro Vieira da Silva Magalhaes, Darin D. Dougherty, Andrew A. Nierenberg, and Natasha Hansen

## Overview

Bipolar disorder (BD) is characterised by periods of elevated and most often episodes of depressed mood. Though mood elevation, or mania, is the hallmark of BD, depression represents the most significant problem for many patients with bipolar disorder. Medication is the first-line treatment for BD but often fails to bring depressed patients to sustained remission.

Findings from a randomised trial within the Systematic Treatment Enhancement Program for Bipolar Disorder (STEP-BD) study suggest that psychotherapy adjunctive to medication can improve depression. The STEP trial examined the efficacy of intensive psychotherapy (IP; 30 sessions of either cognitive behavioural therapy, family-focused therapy, or interpersonal and social rhythm therapy) or collaborative care (CC; 3 sessions of psychoeducation-based treatment) adjunctive to mood-stabilising pharmacotherapy for 293 adults with bipolar depression. Overall, patients in the IP group had significantly higher year-end recovery rates and a shorter time to recovery than the patients in the CC group. Given the variability in response rates to both treatments, in a series of post-hoc analyses of the STEP-BD dataset, we investigated predictors and moderators of treatment response to IP (vs CC) in depressed BD patients.

## Major Findings

Our findings suggest that in the context of the STEP-BD psychotherapy trial, attributional style, illness duration, overall medical burden, and body mass index (BMI) predict a patient's likelihood of recovery from bipolar depression. Attributional style refers to one's process for explaining the causes of events. Extreme pessimistic and optimistic attributions at baseline predicted a lower likelihood of recovery and a longer time until recovery; these findings were independent of initial depression severity, which also conferred a poor prognosis for likelihood and speed of recovery from a depressed episode. Further, extreme attributions predicted a greater likelihood of and shortened time to transition from depression to a (hypo)manic or mixed episode.

Longer illness duration predicted a longer time to recovery; the magnitude of this effect was maintained even after adjusting for variables such as prior depressive and manic episodes, lifetime anxiety, and number of comorbidities. Further, independent of group assignment, number of previous depressive episodes predicted recovery rates. Individuals with fewer prior depressive episodes were more likely to recover and demonstrated a faster recovery time than those with a history of multiple periods of depression. Finally, greater medical burden, defined as the number of lifetime medical conditions, predicted a reduced likelihood of recovery from depression in either intervention.

STEP-BD also included several variables such as comorbid anxiety and number of lifetime depressive episodes that may moderate the effects of psychotherapy on recovery rates and treatment outcomes (i.e., treatment response is different to IP vs CC for patients with that particular moderator variable, or scoring high/low on that particular moderator variable). Specifically, participants with a lifetime comorbid anxiety disorder were more likely to recover in IP relative to CC. While participants with one lifetime comorbid anxiety disorder were more likely to respond to IP relative to CC, there was no difference in response rates between IP and CC for participants with several comorbid anxiety disorders. Participants were most likely to benefit from intensive psychotherapy when they had generalised anxiety disorder (medium to large effect) or post-traumatic stress disorder (small to medium effect). In addition, the number of prior lifetime depressive episodes interacted with treatment group to predict likelihood of recovery; specifically, patients with 10 to 20 prior lifetime depressive episodes were more likely to recover in IP relative to CC, whereas no difference in recovery rates between the two treatment groups was observed for participants with 1 to 9 or 20+ prior depressive episodes.

## Clinical Implications

These findings may be a first step towards the development of more personalised treatments for bipolar depression. For some patients, especially those early in the course of BD and/or with fewer episodes, psychoeducation may be as efficacious as a longer, more intensive psychotherapy whereas the same may not be true for patients who have already experienced more episodes. Viewed through this lens, patients with an extensive illness history may benefit more from a 'palliative' treatment approach centered on illness management, creation of feasible goals, and reducing symptoms rather than psychosocial treatments with a strong emphasis for change. Medical burden can also interfere with treatment prognosis and thus, a treatment strategy emphasising nutrition, wellness, and lifestyle goals may be most beneficial. Extreme attribution styles can be targeted through strategies that enhance cognitive adaptability. Further, findings from STEP-BD surrounding comorbid anxiety inform differential treatments based on presence of a lifetime anxiety disorder, number of anxiety disorders, and specific anxiety disorder diagnosis. In summary, our findings suggest that patients with more depressive episodes may benefit more from IP while for patients with fewer lifetime episodes of depression, CC may be an appropriate first step.

## Future Directions

Though these findings provide some insight into the factors influencing treatment response, more systematic studies are needed to investigate which patient or illness characteristics influence the likelihood of treatment response so that treatment approaches can be better tailored to the specific needs of a particular patient. Recently, we synthesised the approaches to the STEP data using a novel cluster analytic approach that identifies subgroups of individuals who exhibit similarities on a set of variables relative to another subgroup of individuals. These data suggest that especially considering illness course and mood episode history can help determine whether a patient is more likely to respond to brief versus intensive psychosocial treatment. Future research directions could further explore cluster analyses as a method for combining individually identified predictors and moderators of treatment response into a metric that can help guide treatment selection and development.

## Further Readings

Deckersbach, T., Peters, A.T., Sylvia, L., Urdahl, A., Magalhaes, P.V., Otto, M.W., … Nierenberg A.A. (2014). Do comorbid anxiety disorders moderate the effects of psychotherapy for bipolar disorder? *American Journal of Psychiatry, 171*(2), 178–186.

Peters, A., Sylvia, L.G., da Silva Magalhaes, P.V., Miklowitz, D.J., Frank, E., Otto, M.W., … Deckersbach, T. (2014). Age at onset, course of illness and response to psychotherapy in bipolar disorder: Results from the Systematic Treatment Enhancement Program for Bipolar Disorder (STEP-BD). *Psychological Medicine., 44*(16), 3455–3467.

Stange, J.P., Sylvia, L.G., da Silva Magalhaes, P.V., Miklowitz, D.J., Otto, M.W., Frank, E., … Deckersbach, T. (2013). Extreme attributions predict the course of bipolar depression: results from the STEP-BD randomized controlled trial of psychosocial treatment. *Journal of Clinical Psychiatry, 74*(3), 249–255.

# Section 7

Psychosis

Chapter 26

# Improving the implementation fidelity and reach of ACT for complex needs

Hamish J. McLeod, Ross White, and Louise Johns

## Overview

Although effective psychological therapies generally attract high acceptability ratings and are greatly valued by service users, we need to do a much better job of achieving widespread implementation across health service systems. This challenge can be particularly evident where service users have complex needs, such as those related to psychosis. United Kingdom (UK) audit data show that despite clinical guideline stipulations (e.g., from National Institute for Health and Care Excellence [NICE]), the routine implementation of psychological treatments for psychosis such as cognitive-behaviour therapy for psychosis (CBTp) and family therapy reaches less than one tenth of those who could benefit from such therapies. As the third wave of psychological treatment approaches expand into psychosis treatment, psychosis focused adaptations of acceptance and commitment therapy for psychosis (ACTp) will face many of the real world implementation challenges that have diluted the beneficial impacts of CBTp and family therapies. To reduce the avoidable suffering and wasted resources that will accompany ineffective implementation of ACTp, we propose that researchers and clinicians should actively work to understand and address the factors that help bridge the gap between clinical trial data and meaningful clinical impact in real world healthcare settings. Choosing to grapple with these challenges of implementation fidelity now will be a good investment in the future of effective care for complex needs. This chapter outlines how wider work on therapy development and implementation science can inform the next generation of ACTp studies.

## Major Findings

Before considering specific issues relevant to implementing ACTp, we will outline a number of wider issues pertinent to psychological intervention development and therapy trial design that help place the need for implementation research in context. We are in an era where randomised controlled trials (RCTs) have become synonymous with best quality evidence for treatment effectiveness. This evaluation method works well when discriminating between highly replicable medical interventions (e.g., drugs or surgical procedures) and enhanced evidence reporting standards such as the Consolidated Transparent Reporting Trials (CONSORT) guidance have helped to improve the clarity and transparency of published RCT evidence. But psychological therapies are complex interventions with many sources of uncontrolled variance that can interfere with generalisation of findings across contexts. To mitigate this, several frameworks have been published in recent years to help complex intervention researchers convert their treatment insights into a form that will maximise real world implementation. The UK Medical Research Council's complex interventions framework and the Delaware Project from North America help therapy researchers address questions of treatment *implementation*, not just efficacy. The need for a more nuanced understanding of psychosocial intervention implementation has also stimulated extension of the CONSORT statement for trial reporting standards. Clinicians and therapy researchers alike will benefit from using these frameworks to understand future trials of complex interventions so that effective treatments have a greater chance of being implemented in contexts outside of the highly controlled parameters of an RCT.

The ACTp evidence base now comprises several RCTs and a number of uncontrolled intervention studies that provide preliminary evidence of effects on outcomes such as reduced hospital readmission, improved emotional adaptation, self-ratings of functional recovery, and enhanced confidence in managing symptoms such as command hallucinations. The treatment effect sizes are in the medium to large range (Cohen's $d = .31$ to $.86$), particularly when the comparator is standard care. Although the size of these effects are likely to diminish when adjusted for trial quality or when compared to active comparator treatments, there are signs that ACTp is developing an evidence base that gives clinicians and researchers an expanded range of viable treatment choices.

The published ACTp research also allows some preliminary observations about patterns of treatment dose, fidelity, and reach. The dose required to achieve an effect on primary outcomes varies substantially across trials with an average of 15.8 sessions but a wide range from 3 to 20 sessions. Data relevant to reach shows that ACTp has been applied to people with psychosis across the range of chronicity and severity and in different treatment settings from acute admission wards to community based care. The context of most treatment outcome research is high resource settings in high-income countries such as the UK, United States (US), and Australia where there are ACT communities and increased access to training and supervision resources. This speaks to the issue of treatment fidelity and the level of competence needed to ensure that ACTp is delivered at the required standard. To date, we have limited data on how to adequately prepare ACTp therapists and how to monitor treatment adherence. The minimum requirements is similar to existing psychological interventions; therapists need pre-intervention training in the therapy protocol followed by ongoing supervision and review of clinical case work by supervisors with ACT expertise.

### Clinical Implications

Helping people to live well in the presence of challenges presented by psychotic experiences is well within the scope of ACTp's philosophy and goals. But, it is also clear that there is much to learn about how ACTp can be best delivered with fidelity across contexts to people presenting with varying treatment needs. A contextual behavioural science approach to clinical practice and therapy refinement has a good chance of bridging the gap between trial evidence and real world practice. As outlined by Hayes et al. (2013), some ways of developing, refining, and implementing psychological treatments are more effective than others. An immediate task for clinicians and researchers is to create collaborations that maximise the impact of such treatment improvement efforts.

### Future Directions

ACTp will make meaningful progress if clinicians and researchers work together to evaluate and understand the ways that effective techniques, in the right doses, can be delivered to the right people to meet their needs. Intervention studies that use modern frameworks for implementation process evaluation will help surmount barriers to wider penetration of effective care. Instrumentation and measurement improvements will also help (e.g., treatment fidelity scales) as will the use of technology to increase the reach of therapy information and strategies (e.g., via mHealth and ICT delivery platforms). Ultimately, ACTp is well placed to mature into a valuable addition to the range of therapies available to people seeking help with managing the consequences of psychosis.

## Further Readings

Hayes, S.C., Long, D.M., Levin, M.E., & Follette, W.C. (2013). Treatment development: Can we find a better way? *Clinical Psychology Review*, *33*(7), 870–882.

Mayo-Wilson, E., Montgomery, P., Hopewell, S., Macdonald, G., Moher, D., & Grant, S. (2013). Developing a reporting guideline for social and psychological intervention trials. *The British Journal of Psychiatry*, *203*(4), 250–254.

Moore, G.F., Audrey, S., Barker, M., Bond, L., Bonell, C., Hardeman, W., … Baird, J. (2015). Process evaluation of complex interventions: Medical Research Council guidance. *British Medical Journal, 350.* doi: 10.1136/bmj.h1258

Chapter 27

# Emotional processes in understanding and treating psychosis

Hamish J. McLeod, Neil Thomas, Susan L. Rossell, and Andrew Gumley

## Overview

The role of emotion within cognitive-behaviour therapy for psychosis (CBTp) has evolved as treatment research and clinical practice has progressed over the past three decades. For example, early case reports framed emotions such as anxiety as a downstream *consequence* of delusional thinking. Similarly, most CBTp goal setting guidance emphasised that treatment need should follow the distress and interference *caused* by symptoms, not their mere presence. Yet, it has become clearer that emotional dysregulation may act as an upstream driver of psychosis, with the possibility it has a strong role to play in causing distressing mental experiences. These observations have unfolded alongside the emergence of the third wave of behaviour therapy approaches. With this we have seen renewed interest in understanding the mediators and moderators of clinical improvement along with a greater focus on the transdiagnostic processes that govern the development and maintenance of problems of emotion, cognition,

and behaviour. As a result, we now have more refined therapeutic targets (e.g., specific symptom experiences such as
anhedonia), new clinical formulations (e.g., transdiagnostic
accounts of how anxiety processes such as worry affect
symptom development and maintenance), and new treatment
techniques (e.g., mindfulness based approaches). Some of
these trends, findings, and future directions for CBTp are presented in this article.

## Major Findings

CBTp has undergone a remarkable transformation from
something of a curiosity in the early 1990s to its modern day
status as a major branch of applied therapy research. We now
know that talking to people about their hallucinations and
delusions does not make them worse, and in many cases it
may help them to process and make sense of their experiences
in a more adaptive way. We have also learned that there is not
really a monolithic entity that we can call CBTp. The prolifer-
ation of meta-analyses have shown that the family tree of
CBTp has many branches across the dimensions of treatment
target (command hallucinations vs. all symptoms), stage of
illness (early psychosis vs long standing experiences) and style
of intervention (e.g., highly behavioural vs very cognitive).
Outcome data across CBTp trials also shows that a treatment
response can occur in domains not directly targeted as part of
the intervention protocol. For example, secondary outcomes
such as depression and social anxiety can improve even when
these have not been targeted for change. Following these data,
emotional processes have become important targets for intervention in newer generation CBTp protocols. Processes such
as worry, rumination, traumatic memory retrieval, and experiential avoidance are now the focus of empirical testing and
evaluation in experimental work and trial contexts. This work

has also stimulated the adoption of treatment manoeuvres that may have previously been considered irrelevant or too difficult to implement in the context of psychosis (e.g., metacognitive strategies).

## Clinical Implications

Psychological therapies are increasingly recognised as a mandatory component of good quality care for people experiencing psychosis but there is much still to do. First, we need better models of specific problematic experiences faced by people with psychosis. In many ways we are moving away from the era of 'CBT for psychosis' into a more transdiagnostic phase where the processes underpinning specifiable problems are identified and then used to drive problem focused psychological formulations and treatment plans. Prominent emerging transdiagnostic problem targets include suicidality, anhedonia, loss of meaning and purpose, and depressed mood. Traditional psychotic symptoms such as hallucinations and delusions will still warrant therapeutic attention for many people experiencing psychosis; however, the next generation of treatment approaches need to be more closely matched to the processes underpinning these problems and their functional consequences. For instance, while symptom elimination may remain a chosen goal for some people, others may be better served by learning new ways of relating more productively to their mind and living well in the presence of symptoms. Also, while distraction and behavioural coping based strategies may help many people manage harmful symptom experiences in the short term, long term and generalised improvements in functioning will most probably require development of a deeper understanding of ones own mind and its vagaries. The techniques in third wave approaches that shape up more adaptive ways of reacting to our mental experiences focus therapeutic attention on promoting skills that support autonomy, self-determination, and the pursuit of a personally meaningful life.

## Future Directions

The move by the National Institute of Mental Health (NIMH) to determine funding allocations on Research Domain Criteria (RDoC) instead of *Diagnostic and Statistical Manual of Mental Disorders* (DSM) diagnoses has stimulated new conversations about the best way to understand and treat mental health problems. This has helped dissolve arbitrary dichotomies between neurosis and psychosis, and has supported moves toward transdiagnostic approaches to formulation and treatment. However, the RDoC approach has drawn criticism for being overly focused on neuroscience research and reductionist models of illness. Hence, there is a need for robust psychological models that understand psychosis *in context,* and can play a major part in shaping better and more effective care. This endeavour may also be helped by using new concepts such as stratified medicine to drive innovative thinking in understanding mental ill health in a personalised and targeted way. As evidence of these developments, therapy protocols are beginning to emerge that target specific sub-types of symptoms that trouble many people with psychosis such anhedonia, and specific classes of hallucinations. These new applied research efforts will bring us closer to genuinely person-centred care that makes meaningful differences to the lives of those seeking psychological help.

## Further Readings

Hershenberg, R., & Goldfried, M.R. (2015). Implications of RDoC for the research and practice of psychotherapy. *Behavior Therapy, 46,* 155–165.

McCarthy-Jones, S., Thomas, N., Strauss, C., Dodgson, G., Jones, N., Woods, A., ... Sommer, I.E. (2014). Better than mermaids and stray dogs? Subtyping auditory verbal hallucinations and its implications for research and practice. *Schizophrenia Bulletin, 40* (Suppl 4), S275–S284.

Schumann, G., Binder, E.B., Holte, A., de Kloet, E.R., Oedegaard, K.J., Robbins, T.W., ... Wittchen, H.U. (2014). Stratified medicine for mental disorders. *European Neuropsychopharmacology, 24*(1), 5–50.

Section 8

Alcohol and Substance Misuse

Chapter 28

# Beyond CBT: What is the future of alcohol use disorder treatment and prevention?

Matthew J. Gullo, Jason M. Coates, Kiri Patton, and Jason P. Connor

## Overview

Alcohol use disorders (AUD) are among the most common and undertreated mental disorders. Applying *Diagnostic and Statistical Manual of Mental Disorders 5th edition* (DSM-5) diagnostic criteria, approximately one in three men and one in four women will develop an AUD in their lifetime. Cognitive-behaviour therapy (CBT) is an effective psychological treatment, but the first episode of treatment usually takes place long after problems arise and long-term risk of relapse remains high. The field is moving away from head-to-head comparisons of different treatment and prevention packages to focusing on key mechanisms of risk and change, as well as moderators of treatment response. This is the next frontier of addiction science. The goal is to optimise treatment outcomes by tailoring CBT to the individual at a mechanistic level and within the context of the stage of their alcohol use.

## Major Findings

CBT is one of the most efficacious psychological treatments for alcohol use disorder. Theoretically, CBT reduces alcohol use by teaching coping skills for situations that precipitate drinking and improving patient confidence in their ability to resist alcohol in cued situations (*drinking refusal self-efficacy*). This focus is what distinguishes it from alternative treatment approaches that may instead focus on enhancing motivation to reduce drinking (Motivation Enhancement Therapy), or increasing engagement in 12-step self-help groups promoting abstinence (Twelve-Step Facilitation Therapy). It is surprising, then, that these different approaches to treatment produce largely equivalent outcomes. Or, is it?

Much is inferred when the outcomes of one psychological treatment are compared to those of another (or a wait-list control group). If Treatment Package A is found to produce better outcomes than Treatment Package B in a randomised controlled trial (RCT), it is inferred that the specific focus of Treatment Package A is what makes all the difference (e.g., increasing self-efficacy). Similarly, and more frequently, when Treatment Package A and Treatment Package B produce outcomes that do not differ, a common interpretation is that the distinct focus of each is not important for behavior change. Rather, behaviour change is brought about by *common factors* across treatments (e.g., therapeutic alliance). With recent advances in statistical analysis and meta-analytic methods, the weight of evidence is shifting in favour of CBT over other treatment approaches. However, even if such findings stand the test of time, and are replicated in alcohol use disorder treatment specifically, what does this reveal? Not as much as one might think.

The knowledge gained by comparing Treatment Package A to Treatment Package B can only reveal so much about what is actually *causing* a reduction in alcohol use. Even with comprehensive and frequent assessment of putative mechanisms of change during treatment, isolating what module, technique, or interpersonal behaviour produced change in that mechanism is simply not possible. The optimal approach to disentangle putative mechanisms necessarily involves an integrative, translational program of research that extends from basic science to preclinical and clinical (RCT) research studies. These designs will lead to strong inferences about what it is that causes change in drinking behaviour. It will also accelerate theory development and the discovery of new methods to affect drinking behaviour.

To illustrate, consider drinking refusal self-efficacy. Numerous studies point to this construct as one of the most robust predictors of treatment outcome and long-term abstinence. The pervading view is that CBT is the treatment of choice for targeting self-efficacy, based on its theoretical foundation. However, almost any psychological treatment, medication, or placebo could produce an increase in drinking refusal self-efficacy and reduce alcohol use, according to Albert Bandura's *Social Cognitive Theory*. Indeed, recent studies have shown that non-CBT treatments produce increases in refusal self-efficacy. Some have even shown that the effect of therapeutic alliance on alcohol outcome is mediated by drinking refusal self-efficacy. It is now becoming much clearer that there are many different pathways to increasing refusal self-efficacy. Determining the optimal means of increasing self-efficacy cannot be reliably achieved within traditional RCT methodology. The same argument can be applied to any other putative mechanism of change.

Basic scientific and preclinical research on putative mechanisms of change can accelerate treatment innovation. For instance, basic research into the structure, development and correlates of refusal self-efficacy has shown that it exists prior to alcohol onset and is influenced by alcohol outcome expectancies, genetics and personality traits (especially impulsivity). These findings help to outline the pathways through which more distal risk factors ultimately influence alcohol use behaviour. They also provide key targets for early intervention. Human preclinical studies complement this work by testing the causal effect of specific psychological techniques on these targets in the laboratory, and the subsequent impact on alcohol consumption. These techniques can then be integrated with increased confidence into prevention or treatment programs and trialled in an RCT.

## Clinical Implications

Two patients of equivalent severity enter treatment for AUD. Both have been abstinent from alcohol for one week. One patient scores 2 standard deviations above the mean on craving, but close to the mean on drinking refusal self-efficacy. The other patient scores close to the mean on craving, but 2 standard deviations below the mean on refusal self-efficacy. Should they each receive the same treatment with its components delivered in the same order? On what scientific evidence could such a decision be based?

A greater understanding of AUD mechanisms of risk and change will be the key to treatment innovation. Theoretically, some mechanisms will be more responsive to one approach over another - and these relationships will likely be moderated by other important factors (genetics, comorbid psychopathology, medication). Targeted assessment and monitoring of these mechanisms may provide better prognostic information and guide treatment decisions. Similarly, targeted assessment within a prevention context may facilitate early identification of AUD risk and better direct prevention strategies.

## Future Directions

Our understanding of the mechanisms that govern risk and change is becoming increasingly complex. We first need to 'get back to basics' to isolate the effect of specific psychological techniques in the laboratory, and determine what moderates their effectiveness. The field will then be better placed to optimise current intervention packages and develop new ones. As this knowledge base expands, more sophisticated methods will be required to use this wealth of information to aid clinical decision-making. Armed with an array of assessment data, computer-based algorithms often predict treatment outcome better than the treating therapist. This gap will only widen as knowledge of the mechanisms of behaviour change expands. The future of AUD treatment and prevention will not be the selection of Treatment Package A over Treatment Package B, applied to all. Instead, a personalised treatment will be constructed for the individual that consists of a unique combination of components that have been empirically selected after a thorough assessment.

## Further Readings

Magill, M., & Longabaugh, R. (2013). Efficacy combined with specified ingredients: A new direction for empirically supported addiction treatment. *Addiction, 108,* 874–881. doi:10.1111/add.12013

Connor, J.P., Haber, P.S., & Hall, W. D. (2015). Alcohol use disorders. *The Lancet, 387,* 994. doi:10.1016/S0140-6736(15)

Gullo, M.J., Dawe, S., Kambouropoulos, N., Staiger, P.K., & Jackson, C.J. (2010). Alcohol expectancies and drinking refusal self efficacy mediate the association of impulsivity with alcohol misuse. *Alcoholism: Clinical and Experimental Research, 34,* 1386–1399. doi:10.1111/j.1530-0277.2010.01222.x

Chapter 29

# The interplay between emotion and biased cognitive processing in problematic consumption

Lies Notebaert, Henry Austin, Peter J. de Jong, Eva Kemps, Colin MacLeod, and Reinout Wiers

## Overview

People frequently engage in consumption that can negatively impact their physical and mental health, including eating junk food and drinking alcohol. While some do so in ways that are relatively harmless, for others this consumption can become severely problematic. Almost 40% of adults worldwide are now overweight, and thus at increased risk of cardiovascular diseases, diabetes, musculoskeletal disorders, and some cancers. Worldwide, 3.3 million deaths every year result from harmful use of alcohol, which also is a causal factor in a wide range of diseases, injury conditions, and mental and behavioural disorders.

Given these detrimental consequences for individuals and societies, researchers are seeking to identify the processes that underlie problematic consumption. In addition to advancing understanding concerning why people engage in harmful patterns of consumption, identifying the underlying processes will inform the development and refinement of effective public health interventions and clinical procedures that can attenuate problematic consumption.

## Major Findings

Two lines of enquiry can be distinguished in research investigating the processes underlying problematic consumption. The first line has predominantly focused on the contribution of emotional processes, while the second has predominantly focused on the contribution of cognitive processes. Both research lines have produced major insights into the drivers of problematic consumption.

Emotions can be important drivers of problematic food and alcohol consumption. Correlational evidence indicates a link between negative emotion and unhealthy eating, revealing a positive association between increased experience of negative mood and obesity. Relatedly, significant comorbidity exists between eating disorders and affective disorders. Negative mood inductions can increase food craving and consumption, particularly in restrained eaters, and positive mood can have a similar, albeit smaller effect. Emotional processes are similarly implicated in alcohol consumption, and emotionally motivated drinking is an important contributor to problematic alcohol consumption. For example, research has shown that negative mood inductions increase craving in alcohol-dependent patients. In addition, people undergoing addiction treatment often cite heightened emotion as a reason for alcohol use, and such emotionally motivated drinking represents a common pathway to relapse among recovering alcoholics. It is evident, therefore, that emotional processes are important contributors to problematic consumption.

Another line of research has focused on the role played by cognitive processes in driving problematic food and alcohol consumption. Cognitive processes can be assessed using self-report measures, however these measures have poor validity. Therefore researchers have increasingly sought to develop behavioural paradigms capable of indexing specific cognitive processes. A particular focus of this research has been on the role of attentional bias, which in this context is the tendency to preferentially attend to food or alcohol related information, or on approach-avoid motivations, which is the tendency to preferentially approach or avoid food or alcohol-related information. Both of these processes have been implicated in problematic consumption. For example, attentional bias to food-related words is associated with increased hunger, and attentional bias to alcohol-related information is associated with more frequent and heavier drinking. Problematic eaters demonstrate heightened approach motivation to food-related stimuli, and heavy drinkers exhibit heightened approach motivation to alcohol-related stimuli. Prospective studies have shown that early measure of these cognitive processes predict problematic consumption, while manipulation studies have shown that the modification of these cognitive processes can alter problematic consumption. Such findings strongly suggest that these cognitive processes make an important causal contribution to problematic food and alcohol consumption.

While it is recognised that both emotional and cognitive processes contribute to problematic consumption, very little research has sought to examine these processes concurrently. Cross-fertilisation of the expertise developed in each of these two research streams however has created the potential for exciting synergy to enhance our understanding of problematic consumption. Specifically, there is growing evidence to suggest that negative emotion may contribute to problematic consumption via the impact that negative emotion exerts on the cognitive processes that drive such consumption. For example, it has been shown that the induction of negative emotion can increase attentional bias to food images, with a consequent increase in craving of food. In people who report drinking to cope with anxiety, a negative mood induction has been shown to increase attentional bias to alcohol-related words, which is a cognitive bias known to be implicated in increased alcohol consumption. In alcohol-dependent patients, a negative mood induction has been shown to activate memories concerning alcohol-approach motivations, and it is known that heightened alcohol approach-motivation causally contributes to elevated alcohol consumption.

## Clinical Implications

An enhanced understanding of the interplay between emotion and cognition in the determination of problematic consumption, will serve to inform public health initiatives aimed at preventing the development of harmful consumption, and clinical interventions aimed at remediating dysfunctional consumption. Research that illuminates the cognitive pathways through which emotion exerts its impact on consumption may identify additional cognitive targets for change within CBT programs designed to reduce problematic consumption. This work also could have implications concerning how emotional experience may be therapeutically harnessed in CBT programs. For example, if the cognitive processes underlying problematic consumption are activated by specific emotions, then CBT procedures designed to alter these cognitive processes may be more effective when deployed while this emotion is being experienced.

## Future Directions

The interplay between emotion and biased cognitive processing, in the determination of problematic consumption, will be illuminated by future research that makes constructive use of mood induction procedures. Cognitive bias modification procedures, that directly manipulate the cognitive processes triggered by particular emotional states, also will be useful in establishing the functional role such processes play in mediating the impact of emotional states on dysfunctional consumption. The most powerful models of emotionally-motived consumption will explain not only how differences in emotional disposition exert their influence on consumption, but also will identify the factors that give rise to these differences in emotional disposition. Thus, future research that advances understanding of individual differences in emotional disposition, while also illuminating how differing emotional experiences trigger the cognitive processes known to drive maladaptive consumption, can be expected to deliver the greatest benefits in terms of explaining why some people, more than others, tend to engage in problematic patterns of consumption.

## Further Readings

Cousijn, J., Luijten, M., & Wiers, R.W. (2014). Mechanisms underlying alcohol-approach action tendencies: The role of emotional primes and drinking motives. *Frontiers in Psychiatry, 5,* 44.

Hepworth, R., Mogg, K., Brignell, C., & Bradley, B.P. (2010). Negative mood increases selective attention to food cues and subjective appetite. *Appetite, 54,* 134–142.

Obasi, E. M., Brooks, J. J., & Cavanagh, L. (2016). The relationship between psychological distress, negative cognitions, and expectancies on problem drinking: Exploring a growing problem among university students. *Behavior Modification, 40*(1–2), 51–69.

Section 9

Health and Chronic Medical Disorders

Chapter 30

# Motivational interviewing and CBT to improve health and wellbeing

Amanda L. Baker, Leanne Hides, Peter J. Kelly, Frances Kay-Lambkin, Yasmina Nasstasia, and Max Birchwood

## Overview

Large epidemiological studies in the last two decades have shown that many people in the community experience mental health and substance use problems in their lifetime and, and they commonly co-occur. Although co-existing mental health and substance use problems are very common, psychological treatments for these problems have traditionally been delivered separately in different services. Consequently, many people with co-existing disorders do not receive adequate treatment, resulting in worse treatment outcomes, including increased rates of relapse, medication use and health care costs. In the longer term, mental health problems (e.g., depression) and substance use problems (e.g., smoking) are themselves associated with increased rates of cardiovascular and respiratory diseases and cancer. There is a life expectancy gap of around 20 years between people living with mental health and substance use problems versus those not experiencing such problems. The first National Mental Health

Report Card in Australia in 2012 called the physical health status of people living with a mental health condition a 'national disgrace'. The report called upon researchers and clinicians to better address the physical health of people with mental health and substance use problems. Despite burgeoning research linking these comorbidities, treatment services remain siloed into separate delivery systems for mental ill health, substance misuse and physical ill health, and for young people versus adults.

## Major Findings

Our group has begun to investigate how best we can apply healthy lifestyles approaches, motivational interviewing (MI) and cognitive-behaviour therapy (CBT) to the settings in which we work. With special expertise in working with young people, Leanne Hides' research has found significant relationships between physical activity, mental wellbeing and psychological distress. She is also collaborating on a project with Amanda Baker and Yasmina Nasstasia and colleagues piloting MI and an exercise intervention among young people with major depressive disorder. Amanda Baker has led the development of a healthy lifestyles intervention for smokers with psychotic disorders and has found that a telephone delivered intervention was just as effective as face-to-face delivery. Peter Kelly, Frances Kay-Lambkin and their respective colleagues have furthered developed this MI/CBT healthy lifestyles framework applying it in substance abuse residential rehabilitation and online among people with mental ill health.

## Clinical Implications

MI/CBT using a healthy lifestyles framework for co-existing mental health and substance use issues represents an important new innovation in early intervention and treatment. A healthy lifestyles framework reduces stigma, is more appealing to people, as it encourages small changes across a number of health behaviours and avoids prematurely focusing on substance misuse, which may elicit resistance. Self-efficacy for behaviour change is thus enhanced and as behaviour change accrues across health behaviours, the overall outcome may be reduction in risk for chronic physical ill health and enhancement of wellbeing. Healthy lifestyles MI/CBT can be employed by health practitioners in various settings such as primary care, and youth and adult mental health and substance use treatment settings to address comorbidity.

Healthy lifestyles MI/CBT uses all the principles and concepts of MI/CBT, eliciting the person's presenting concerns, identifying values held most dearly and, with permission from the person, providing information and feedback about how various health behaviours might be linked with their presenting concerns. Health behaviours covered will depend on the time available. Where time is short, we suggest providing a rationale for screening the four key behaviours associated with most chronic diseases: smoking, alcohol misuse, low fibre diet and physical inactivity. For example, if the person is presenting with complaints of low mood and poor sleep, offering a rationale like 'I can hear how much the low mood and poor sleep distresses you, especially as your studies are so important. I'd like us both to understand more about your mood and sleep before we consider how we might go about improving them. One of the things we might think about is to keep a diary this week to find out when you feel better, when you feel worst and what you are doing at those times. Can I tell you something about what many people I see find effects their mood and sleep? Well, things like your levels of activity, how well you eat, and also drinking coffee, and alcohol and smoking can have a big effect. Can we spend a little time just checking in about those things?' This approach places stigmatised behaviours such as smoking and alcohol consumption alongside more socially acceptable behaviours and places them within a context relevant to the person's values and goals. In this example, the person may choose to monitor their smoking and alcohol consumption along with their other activities in their diary, thus potentially linking these with mood and sleep problems along with low levels of pleasant activity. Fruit and vegetable consumption per day is an easy way to start people thinking about their diet, so asking them to monitor whether they have consumed the recommended levels of daily fruit and vegetables can be helpful. We have found that if people are not good diarists, a 24 hour snapshot taken at the beginning of each session can help the development of a formulation involving health behaviours.

When a collaborative formulation has been developed and if multiple sessions are planned, this can be further elaborated as more information is gained about health behaviours and how they link to presenting concerns. The intervention allows individuals to select their own goals and to work on one or more behaviours at any time. There is accumulating evidence that multiple health behaviour change is feasible, acceptable and effective and that it can have positive effects on mental health, substance misuse and physical health and well-being.

## Future Directions

In summary, a healthy lifestyles MI/CBT approach to people with mental and substance use problems is promising. Face-to-face, telephone, group and internet interventions appear potentially beneficial. Further research among larger samples including young people and people attending primary care, mental health or substance use treatment settings, are required to establish the efficacy of such an approach. Areas in which further research may be particularly beneficial, in which current evidence for treatment efficacy is limited, includes cannabis use among people with mental health and/or substance use problems and for people who use methamphetamine, who commonly experience distressing mental and physical health issues.

## Further Readings

Baker, A.L., Turner, A., Kelly, P., Spring, B., Callister, R., Woodcock, K ... Lewin, T.J. (2014). 'Better Health Choices' by telephone: A feasibility trial of improving diet and physical activity in people diagnosed with psychotic disorders. *Psychiatry Research, 220,* 63–70. doi:10.1016/j.psychres.2014.06.035

Baker, A., Hiles, S., Thornton, L., Searl, A., Kelly, P., & Kay-Lambkin, F. (2013). From comorbidity to multiple health behaviour change. In W. Mistral (Ed.), *Emerging perspectives on substance misuse,* (pp. 152–169). Chichester, England: Wiley-Blackwell.

Baker, A., Callister, R., Kelly, P., & Kypri, K. (2012). 'Do more, smoke less!' Harm reduction in action for smokers with mental health/substance use problems who cannot or will not quit. *Drug and Alcohol Review, 31(5),* 714-717. doi:10.1111/j.1465-3362.2012.00461.x

Chapter 31

# Navigating the impact of serious illness across the family system using evidence-based therapeutic approaches

U.M. Sansom-Daly, Brittany C. McGill, Nadine A. Kasparian, Pandora Patterson, Frank Muscara, and Claire E. Wakefield

## Overview

Each year, more than 1,200 Australian parents are told their child or adolescent has cancer, another 21,000 young people receive the news that their parent has cancer, while about 1 in 100 infants are diagnosed with some form of congenital heart disease. Fortunately, due to medical advances, most survive these conditions. Beyond medical survival, however, the impact of a serious illness can have far-reaching effects that ripple through the family system. Illness stressors can challenge young peoples' emerging coping skills during the peak years of onset for mental health disorders. Similarly, parents grappling with their child's serious illness may experience complex psychological responses, including bonding and parenting difficulties, and poor mental health outcomes. Without evidence-based intervention, the psychological aftereffects of serious illness can last for years beyond diagnosis and treatment.

## Major Findings

Empirical understanding of psychological distress in the context of life-threatening and chronic illness has long been conceptualised in terms of its impact across the family system. Among adults with a serious illness, carers (often partners) can experience distress that equals, if not exceeds, that of the patient. This pattern is also observed in child and adolescent offspring of seriously unwell adults. Similarly, parents of children with serious illness show poor psychological outcomes that again can eclipse those of their unwell child. The rippling of illness-related distress through the extended family system also leaves several less visible subgroups (such as siblings and grandparents) vulnerable to falling 'between the cracks' in terms of clinical assessment and provision of evidence-based interventions.

We have trialled a series of evidence-based interventions to target a spectrum of illness-related concerns in the family system, including: 'Truce', 'Cascade' and 'Recapture Life', described below.

In response to the psychological burden associated with an adolescent and young adults (AYA) parent's cancer diagnosis, CanTeen[1] developed *Truce*, a manualised, Acceptance and Commitment Therapy (ACT)-based intervention. The aim of ACT is to decrease experiential avoidance and increase psychological flexibility; allowing for the creation of a full and meaningful life, while accepting the pain that life inevitably brings (such as illness in a loved-one). Over seven

---

[1] CanTeen is an Australian charity that provides psychosocial support to 12 to 24 year olds who have cancer, have a sibling or parent with cancer, or have had a family member die from cancer.

weeks, young people meet face-to-face for approximately two hours learning skills to nurture resilience in living with the reality of their parent's cancer. Parents receive psycho-education about the cancer impact on their child and take part in the sixth session of the program. Preliminary evaluation results are promising with young people strongly engaging with the program, reductions in distress, and increased use of mindfulness.

Identifying and treating illness-related distress once the patient is no longer engaged directly with the hospital system presents another challenge. Responding to patient isolation and geographical barriers to care, we developed two online trans-diagnostic, manualised, CBT-based interventions at the Sydney Children's Hospital to assist AYA cancer survivors and parents of paediatric cancer survivors to cultivate adaptive coping skills to adjust to their (child's) early survivorship period. The interventions, called 'ReCaPTure LiFe' (Resilience and Coping skills for young People to Live well Following cancer) and 'CASCAdE' (Cope, Adapt, Survive: Life after CAncEr), use a group-based format, led by a psychologist and delivered using online videoconferencing, to ameliorate post-cancer distress and improve quality of life. Despite the well-acknowledged challenges associated with delivering psychological interventions online, the results from these programs are promising. Strong feasibility and acceptability results have emerged from the Cascade pilot, and early evidence suggests that Recapture Life reduces psychological distress, particularly anxiety.

Despite these promising results, we need to better understand the unique psychological mechanisms underpinning the distress seen in various patient groups; for example, the sense of 'biographical disruption' experienced by AYA cancer patients/survivors. Recent non-clinical, experimental studies using healthy AYAs with some degree of health anxiety have shown that engaging in ruminative thinking - one process known to underpin adverse outcomes among disorders such as depression — leads young people with higher health anxiety to generate more 'over-general' illness-related future imaginings, as well as more illness-concerned 'self-defining memories'. These results suggest that even among physically well individuals susceptible to illness concerns, rumination may have the capacity to negatively impact both the content and nature of autobiographical future thinking. Early work by our group at the University of New South Wales translating these findings to young people with cancer using the 'life narratives' paradigm appears to similarly indicate that young people with cancer are less able to imagine their future lives in a specific way, relative to their healthy counterparts.

As another example, fetal diagnosis of congenital heart disease often precipitates an emotional crisis for expectant parents and can lead to long-term psychosocial difficulties. Threats to the health of the fetus have long been recognised as an important risk factor for psychiatric disturbance during pregnancy, which in turn indicates a higher risk of ongoing psychiatric disorders postpartum. Studies show that antenatal screening leading to the detection of a fetal abnormality can result in increased maternal and paternal anxiety during pregnancy, as well as symptoms of depression and traumatic stress, and that the severity of these symptoms may be markedly underestimated by healthcare providers. Identification of a problem in utero amplifies an anxiety often experienced by women during pregnancy — that of bearing an unhealthy child. This knowledge, with its uncertainty of outcome, may interfere with parents' emotional preparation for the arrival of their baby, as well as subsequent parent-child bonding. For expectant parents, grief and fear are coupled with concerns about delivery plans, the infant's heart surgery and overall future quality of life.

## Clinical Implications

It is imperative that the healthcare team conceptualise serious illness as a stressor, the psychological impact of which can spread through the family system. Regular patient and family distress screening is indicated. The healthcare team should consider ways to support patients and their families not only during acute treatment, but in the transition from home to hospital, and in the long-term management of chronic illness.

## Future Directions

We need to better understand the mechanisms underlying illness-related distress, and continue efforts to foster trans-diagnostic models of treatment. Evaluation of evidence-based interventions, as in many other areas of psychology, is hindered by poorly designed trials that do not utilise an active control group. Online interventions in particular require further rigorous evaluation, taking into consideration important factors such as therapeutic alliance and cost-effectiveness.

## Further Readings

Hearps, S.J., McCarthy, M.C., Muscara, F., Hearps, S.J., Burke, K., Jones, B., & Anderson, V.A. (2014). Psychosocial risk in families of infants undergoing surgery for a serious congenital heart disease. *Cardiology in the Young, 24*(4), 632–639. doi: 10.1017/S1047951113000760

Patterson, P., McDonald, F.E., Ciarrochi, J., Hayes, L., Tracey, D., Wakefield, C.E., & White, K. (2015). A study protocol for Truce: a pragmatic controlled trial of a seven-week acceptance and commitment therapy program for young people who have a parent with cancer. *BMC Psychology, 3*(1), 1. doi: 10.1186/s40359-015-0087-y

Sansom-Daly, U.M., Wakefield, C.E., Bryant, R.A., Butow, P., Sawyer, S., Patterson, P., ... Cohn, R.J. (2012). Online group-based cognitive-behavioural therapy for adolescents and young adults after cancer treatment: a multicenter randomised controlled trial of Recapture Life-AYA. *BMC Cancer, 12*, 339. doi: 10.1186/1471-2407-12-339

Chapter 32

# Depression and anxiety following traumatic brain injury: Can these high prevalence disorders be effectively treated using adapted cognitive behavioural therapy?

Jennie Ponsford, Dana Wong, Adam McKay, Yvette Alway, Kerrie Haines, Nicole K Lee, Marina Downing, and Meaghan L. O'Donnell

## Overview

The majority of individuals with a traumatic brain injury (TBI) experience a psychiatric disorder following their injury. These disorders are significantly associated with disability, unemployment, familial strain, and health care utilisation. Therefore, identification and implementation of effective treatments is crucial. However, cognitive impairments resulting from TBI make psychological treatments such as cognitive-behaviour therapy (CBT) difficult to deliver due to demands on memory, metacognitive awareness and problem solving. This chapter will address the question of whether CBT adapted to compensate for cognitive impairments can be effective in reducing depression and anxiety in people with TBI, from identification of the problems, through to evidence of treatment efficacy and evaluation clinical translation methods.

## Major Findings

In our recent longitudinal prospective study, 161 individuals with moderate to severe TBI were evaluated for DSM-IV Axis I psychiatric disorders over the first 5 years following their injury. Findings confirmed a high frequency of psychiatric disorders following TBI, with 75.2% receiving one or more psychiatric diagnosis during the first 5 years, and 12-month frequencies higher than in the Australian general population up to the fourth year post-injury. Mood and anxiety disorders were most common, presenting comorbidly in approximately three in four cases. While most common where there was a history of pre-injury psychiatric problems, these disorders emerged in more than 40% of those without a history of the disorder prior to injury. Although many cases received depression and anxiety disorder *not otherwise specified* diagnoses, major depressive disorder and posttraumatic stress disorder (PTSD) were the most common classifiable diagnoses and were frequently chronic and recurrent in course. As early intervention has the potential to shorten disorder duration and reduce likelihood of reoccurrence, there is a need to strengthen the evidence base for effective psychological treatments in TBI populations.

There is growing support for the efficacy of CBT in treating anxiety and depression following brain injury. However, it is clear that CBT needs to be adapted to be suitable for individuals with significant cognitive impairments such as difficulties with new learning, working memory, cognitive flexibility, and emotion regulation. In a recent randomised controlled trial (RCT) involving 75 individuals with anxiety and/or depression following TBI we found manualised CBT, which was adapted to accommodate cognitive impairments, and incorporated post-treatment booster sessions, was effective in alleviating anxiety and depressive symptoms, relative to waitlist controls. Key modifications to CBT made in this intervention included strategies for enhancing learning of CBT skills, such as use of repetition, simplified materials, incremental learning, handouts, use of therapy partners, and booster sessions. Behavioural strategies were often a core focus of treatment while significant therapist guidance and support was often required for identifying and adapting unhelpful automatic thoughts and beliefs. Significant gains relative to a control group receiving treatment as usual emerged only gradually over several months post-intervention and following three booster sessions.

Given our finding that adapted CBT was effective in reducing depression and anxiety symptoms in people with TBI, we wanted to translate this manualised intervention into broader clinical practice. We have recently been evaluating the impact of attending a day-long workshop and receiving individual supervision on therapist competence in giving adapted CBT to individuals with anxiety and depression following a brain injury. The workshop included didactic content, case examples, experiential exercises, role plays, and videos of adapted CBT in action. Individual supervision sessions were focused on therapists' audio recordings of adapted CBT sessions conducted within their workplace. Initial findings suggest that workshop attendance led to increases in therapists' self-ratings of basic and specific adapted CBT competencies. Data assessing the additional effect of individual supervision are still being collected; however, qualitatively, therapist feedback to date suggests that supervision has had a positive impact on their competence in delivering adapted

CBT, particularly with regard to managing process issues such as containment and session structure.

## Clinical Implications

The high frequency of psychiatric disorders, particularly depression and anxiety, highlights a need for routine psychiatric screening for individuals following TBI. Those with psychiatric disorders should be directed to clinicians with dual expertise in these conditions (e.g., neuropsychiatrists, specialised clinical psychologists or neuropsychologists) so treatment can be tailored to accommodate cognitive impairment in psychological therapy and potential for side effects in psychopharmacological management. CBT adapted for people with brain injury can alleviate anxiety and depression symptoms. Modified CBT needs to adopt principles to support learning of CBT, target key issues that are common in people with TBI and include booster sessions to consolidate and maintain therapeutic gains. Preliminary evidence suggests that training therapists in CBT adapted for TBI is most effective when interactive workshop attendance is combined with individual supervision.

## Future Directions

There is a need for much further research investigating the effectiveness, of CBT and other cognitive therapies in the TBI population, particularly identifying effective elements and adaptations of therapy and most effective means of implementing them in clinical practice.

## Further Readings

Alway, Y., Gould, K.R, Johnston, L., McKenzie, D., Ponsford, J. (2016). A prospective examination of Axis I psychiatric disorders in the first 5 years following moderate to severe traumatic brain injury. *Psychological Medicine, 46*(6), pp. 1331–1341.

Ponsford, J., Lee, N.K., Wong, D., Mckay, A., Haines, K., Alway, Y., ... O'Donnell, M.L. (2016). Efficacy of motivational interviewing and cognitive behavioral therapy for anxiety and depression symptoms following traumatic brain injury. *Psychological Medicine, 46*(5), pp.1079–1090.

Ponsford, J., Sloan, S., & Snow, P. (2012). *Traumatic brain injury: rehabilitation for everyday adaptive living* (2nd ed.). Hove, England: Psychology Press.

Chapter 33

# Information processing and stuttering

Robyn Lowe, Mark Onslow, Ann Packman, Sue O'Brian, and Ross G. Menzies

## Overview

Stuttering is a speech disorder that involves involuntary interruptions to speech production, reducing the capacity to communicate effectively. Stuttering affects 1% to 2% of adults. Up to two-thirds of treatment-seeking adults who stutter suffer from social anxiety disorder (SAD). According to contemporary cognitive models of SAD, the disorder is maintained by behaviours or internal cognitive processes when anxiety is aroused within feared social situations. One such process is a shift of attentional focus to excessive self-monitoring. That process can impair access to accurate feedback from the social environment. Those with SAD use information obtained from self-monitoring to generate an image or impression of how they think they appear to others. Images and impressions tend to be negative, distorted and viewed from the observer perspective, as if looking back at the self from the perspective of others. Another feature of SAD is the use of safety behaviours–cognitive processes or behaviours used in an attempt to prevent feared outcomes such as negative evaluation from others. In debilitating states of SAD, safety behaviours prevent fear extinction and anxiety is maintained. This article reports on recent research with those who stutter drawing on cognitive models of SAD.

## Major Findings

The most empirically based and effective treatment for stuttering with adults is speech restructuring. Speech restructuring involves teaching clients to control their stuttering using a novel speech technique. However, two thirds of clients are unable to maintain fluency after treatment. A recent seminal report published by the first author's research group provides an explanation for that effect. In that study, adults who stutter diagnosed with one or more mental health disorders failed to maintain the benefits of their speech treatment. In other words, only the third of participants without a mental health disorder were able to maintain the benefits of their speech treatment. In light of those findings it is critical to identify the factors that maintain mental health disorders and anxiety with those who stutter.

Our research group has shown with direct observation of eye gaze using eye tracking that, compared to fluent speakers, those who stutter look less toward audience members while giving a speech. Further evidence of self-focused attention has been demonstrated by an association between reduced eye gaze, increased anxiety, and negative self-perceptions.

Those who stutter have been shown to experience intrusive mental imagery. Evidence from our research has shown that those who stutter compared to fluent speakers are more likely to experience distorted, negative and observer perspective images and impressions.

It is well documented from self-reports and emerging evidence that those who stutter engage in behaviours in anticipation of stuttering or in an attempt to deal with stuttering. Our research has shown that, during routine treatment for stuttering, speech-language pathologists recommended that their clients use behaviours that might under certain circumstances be considered safety behaviours. More recent results suggest that the negative effects of safety behaviors known to occur with SAD may also apply to those who stutter.

Recent research has used the Stroop and dot probe tasks to assess attention with those who stutter. There is some suggestion of similar attentional processing biases as found with SAD using the Stroop task however that does not appear to be the case using the dot-probe task. Interpretation of results with those who stutter, as with SAD, needs to take into account the limitations of those task requirements and the nature of attention assessed.

**Clinical Implications**

It is clinically important that many adults who stutter display the same maladaptive information processing and behaviours that occur with those who have SAD; they appear to neglect positive social cues during social interactions that could disconfirm negative beliefs and fears, they recall faulty images and engage in certain behaviours in anticipation or as a result of their stuttering. Those emerging results may begin to explain why morbid fear of embarrassment and humiliation can persist with those who stutter. Further, attentional processes and maladaptive behavioural responses may contribute to impaired speech treatment efficacy. This poses significant implications for the person who stutters and those who provide treatment services.

Speech treatment involving restructuring requires significant cognitive resources for the client to implement. Internal cognitive processes and safety behaviours may impact on attentional resources available to implement speech treatment techniques.

Speech treatment programs could incorporate procedures to increase attention to social cues. It will be useful to identify faulty imagery which may then be targeted by re-scripting memories. Finally, it will be important to identify the use of safety behaviours by exploring threat cues. The findings of biased attentional processes and maladaptive behavioural responses with those who stutter indicate for them the potential benefits of cognitive behaviour therapy. Evidence has demonstrated that cognitive behaviour therapy with stuttering patients reverses SAD diagnoses and improves overall psychological functioning.

The goal of future research is to improve the lives of those who stutter by finding effective ways to alleviate their mental health distress and to improve their speech treatment outcomes. The outcomes of that research will inform the development of treatment procedures that may be an adjunct to traditional speech treatment or may inform the development of more effective treatments.

## Future Directions

One line of potential enquiry is the use of oxytocin. Oxytocin is an important chemical modulator of social behaviour. Nasal spray administration of oxytocin enhances eye gaze, improves the encoding and recall of faces, and facilitates trust behaviour and the detection of positive social cues. Combined with speech treatment, oxytocin may increase access to positive feedback from social interactions, thereby decreasing anxiety.

Another potential research path is attention training. This involves training attention toward desirable targets such as positive faces, or away from undesirable targets such as negative faces. With SAD attentional training corrects attentional biases, is associated with anxiety reduction and the reversal of DSM-V diagnoses. Typically patients undergo training with computer-based programs which could be used with those who stutter, however, it will be of interest to explore the effect of direct instruction. Continued research exploring information processing with those who stutter is needed.

## Further Readings

Clark, D.M., & Wells, A. (1995). A cognitive model of social phobia. In R.G. Heimberg, M. R. Liebowitz, D.A. Hope, & F.R. Schneier (Eds.), *Social phobia: Diagnosis, assessment, and treatment* (pp. 69–93). New York, NY: Guilford Press.

Menzies, R., O'Brian, S., Onslow, M., Packman, A., St Clare, T., & Block, S. (2008). An experimental clinical trial of a cognitive-behavior therapy package for chronic stuttering. *Journal of Speech, Language, and Hearing Research, 51*, 1451–1464.

Iverach, L., & Rapee, R. M. (2014). Social anxiety disorder and stuttering: Current status and future directions. *Journal of Fluency Disorders, 40*, 69–82.

Chapter 34

# Behavioural and cognitive treatments for children, adolescents and adults who stutter

Mark Onslow, Robyn Lowe, Ross G. Menzies, and Anthony Gunn

## Overview

Stuttering is a common speech disorder that begins unexpect-edly during the pre-school years after a period of normal speech and language development. Stuttering is physically dis-figuring with repetitions of sounds and words, 'blocks' of the speech mechanism, and tic-like extraneous movements. If it persists past the pre-school years, stuttering can become intractable and be associated with reduced educational and occupational attainment, and a range of associated mental health problems. Stuttering has been shown to affect quality of life as adversely as life-threatening conditions such as neu-rotrauma and coronary heart disease. Stuttering reduces speech output. In severe cases, speech output can be less than a quarter of peers. Social anxiety is common among those pre-senting to speech clinics, with 40% to 60% of cases diagnosed with social anxiety disorder.

## Major Findings

A team led by researchers at the Australian Stuttering Research Centre developed an early intervention for pre-schoolers, known as the Lidcombe Program. The speech pathologist teaches the parent how to present three verbal contingencies for the child's stutter-free speech and two verbal contingencies for stuttering. Parents administer the verbal contingencies when conversing with the child during everyday situations. An example of a verbal contingency for stuttering is 'I heard a bumpy word there, can you try to say that again?'.

Five successful randomised trials of the Lidcombe Program have been published. A realistic clinical expectation from the treatment is no stuttering or nearly no stuttering that is sustained for the long-term in most cases. There is translational evidence that the results of clinical trials can be obtained in community speech pathology clinics. Work has begun to develop a standalone Internet version of the treatment that parents can use without needing to consult a speech pathologist.

For adolescents and adults who stutter, there have been many clinical trials reported of a treatment technique known as speech restructuring. Clients learn to speak with a novel speech pattern to control stuttering, initially in a slow and unnatural manner. Eventually, they learn to use this technique to sound as natural as possible while still controlling their stuttering.

The Camperdown Program is one of many speech restructuring treatments available for adolescent and adult clients who stutter. It was developed by the Australian Stuttering Research Centre team. After initial trial development a randomised trial has confirmed its efficacy. The Camperdown Program provides some advances on previous versions of this treatment style. Notably, it requires around one fifth of the treatment times required of other speech restructuring treatments. A standalone Internet version of the Camperdown Program has been developed, and two preliminary trials have been encouraging. In the most recent trial, five of 20 participants (25%) completed all phases of the Internet treatment, and four of them reduced their stuttering by more than 50%

With so many adult clients presenting to speech clinics with anxiety-related mental health problems, there was a need for a cognitive-behaviour therapy (CBT) package designed specifically for their needs. Such a package was designed based on stuttering-specific mental health assessments developed for this clinical population. Those assessments are used to guide application of standard CBT domains derived from the Clark and Wells model of social anxiety. Preliminary trials and a randomised trial showed that it improved Global Assessment of Functioning, reduced speaking situation avoidance, and removed diagnoses of social anxiety disorder.

A standalone internet treatment has been developed for adult stuttering clients who might benefit from CBT. The treatment website — CBTPsych — requires no contact from a clinician and advances existing mental health management websites by giving a more human feel to the clinical experience by means of voices and images of a man and woman clinical psychologist who engage the user. CBTPsych comprises seven modules that cover standard CBT domains, and users are required to complete each module before proceeding to the next. Preliminary clinical trials show post-treatment mental health improvements similar to those obtained in clinic with a clinical psychologist, and compliance rates superior to other reports of self-direct mental health interventions. The most recent trial of CBTPsych — in review at the time of writing — involved several hundred adult participants from 23 countries.

The onset of social anxiety disorder typically is during early adolescence. Hence, development of a version of CBTPsych for adolescents who stutter is potentially useful. Access to the Internet with laptop, tablet and smartphone devices is now a routine part of the lives of many adolescents. The Australian Stuttering Research Centre team has developed a beta version of CBTPsych for adolescents. Modifications for that age group include use of humour, science trivia, and useless facts. Additionally, adolescents can choose their clinician. Post-trial interviews with participants so far suggest adequate levels of engagement, and positive responses to the design of the site. The team is currently working on a controlled trial to establish the effectiveness of the program.

## Clinical Implications

Research during the past decade has revealed a need for mental health management for many who present to speech pathologists for stuttering treatment. For the speech pathology profession, then, the development of specific CBT techniques for that client group and the CBTPsych website are watershed developments. They foreshadow the possibility that speech pathologists will, without any clinical psychology training, be able to provide a first line of mental health intervention to supplement their speech interventions with adolescent and adult clients who stutter.

## Future Directions

A common theme across all treatments discussed is the development of standalone Internet versions of them that do not require a clinician. The Australian Stuttering Research Centre team has planned continued development of those internet treatments: the Lidcombe Program and Camperdown

Program for stuttering control with children and adults, and CBTPsych for mental health intervention with adults and adolescents who stutter. We are planning randomised trials to establish the effect sizes of those Internet treatments in comparison to their in-clinic counterparts. Ultimately, we project that standalone Internet treatments will be a cost effective first step in stepped care for children and adults who stutter.

## Further Readings

Helgadottir, F.D., Menzies, R., Onslow, M., Packman, A., & O'Brian, S. (2009). Online CBT I: Bridging the gap between Eliza and modern online CBT treatment packages. *Behaviour Change, 26,* 245–253.

O'Brian, S., Carey, B., Lowe, R., Onslow, M., Packman, A., & Cream, A. (2015). *The Camperdown Program Stuttering Treatment Guide.* Retrieved from http://sydney.edu.au/health-sciences/asrc/docs/cp_treatment_guide_2015.pdf

Packman, A., Onslow, M., Webber, M., Harrison, E., Arnott, S., Bridgman, K., … Lloyd, W. (2015). *The Lidcombe Program treatment guide.* Retrieved from http://sydney.edu.au/health-sciences/asrc/docs/lp_treatment_guide_2015.pdf

# Section 10

## Comorbidity

Chapter 35

# Cognitive-behaviour therapy for adults with obsessive-compulsive disorder and autism spectrum disorder: Influence of comorbidity and improvement of treatment outcomes

Akiko Nakagawa, Junichiro Kanazawa, Fumiyo Oshima, and Aki Tsuchiyagito

## Overview

Obsessive-compulsive disorder (OCD) is heterogeneous in its clinical features and continues to be known as one of the most debilitating conditions among all physical and mental illnesses. In recent years, the comorbidity of OCD and autism spectrum disorder (ASD) and OCD-related disorders have been highlighted. In addition to severe cases of OCD, mild cases may be subtyped by the autistic dimension. There are, however, few studies that have adequately investigated and detailed this subject. The elucidation of the influence of comorbid ASD on OCD and related disorders with respect to their clinical features and treatment is important for improving the effectiveness of cognitive-behaviour therapy (CBT) in these patients, and therefore may require adaptation.

## Major Findings

The mechanisms of response to treatment and maintenance of treatment benefits are influenced by comorbid ASD in OCD. We found that the presence of comorbid ASD significantly affected both treatment and follow-up outcomes in patients with OCD. The OCD with ASD group showed higher scores than the OCD without ASD group on the main outcome scale (Yale-Brown Obsessive Compulsive Scale [Y-BOCS]) at mid-treatment, post-treatment and after 7 to 8 years of follow-up.

In addition, at pre-treatment, the OCD with ASD group showed higher scores for 'Ordering' and 'Hoarding' symptoms than the OCD without ASD group on the symptom dimensional scale for OCD. In our other clinical study, hoarding disorder presented with comorbid neurodevelopmental disorders (ADHD and ASD). Based on the analysis of data from interviews, we hypothesised that there are two types of comorbidities of hoarding and neurodevelopmental disorders: ADHD-type hoarding and ASD-type hoarding. Of these, the ASD type seems to be more easily affected by the mental state of the patients.

Finally, we investigated the effectiveness of newly developed treatment procedures in patients having OCD with comorbid ASD, and we present 'schema therapy' (ST) as a possible treatment option for these patients.

ST, developed by Young, might be an effective treatment for patients with OCD and comorbid ASD. ST was specifically developed for patients who did not show an optimal treatment response to traditional CBT. According to ST, early maladaptive schemas (EMSs) are defined as self-perpetuating, dysfunctional cognitive patterns that emerge from unmet basic needs and traumatic experiences during childhood. In our previous research, we found that autism spectrum traits in typically developing adults affect the mental health status via EMSs. According to Thiel, the use of ST elements in the treatment of OCD may specifically help treat identified negative EMS predictors and, subsequently, further improve the treatment outcome. We are currently planning a combination of CBT and ST for the treatment of patients with OCD and comorbid ASD.

## Clinical Implications

These results indicate that comorbid ASD predicts poor treatment and follow-up outcomes of CBT for OCD. This may be a result of differences in the underlying mechanism of obsessive-compulsive (OC) symptoms with and without comorbid ASD. Further, ASD might influence OC symptoms, particularly hoarding because of the ASD characteristics. People who hoard have strong urges to save items or information, and this strong urges might be related to the compulsiveness in OCD and the lack of flexibility in ASD. The hypotheses regarding these differences need to be examined and applied in CBT for patients with OCD and comorbid ASD. ASD diagnosis is important for understanding the clinical and psychosocial features of and treatment responses in OCD, thereby improving the efficacy of CBT for OCD; further, ST along with CBT is a potential treatment option.

## Future Directions

OCD itself seems to be highly heterogeneous and so does OCD with ASD. In previous studies on OC symptoms in ASD, patients showed a repeated performance to relieve incompleteness or a repetitive movement-like mannerism as one the characteristics of ASD without any obsessive thoughts and little insight for them (motoric type). However, in patients having OCD with ASD, particularly high-functioning patients, obsession evokes fear/anxiety, and compulsion is performed to reduce the fear/anxiety (cognitive type). Patients having OCD with ASD tend to have both types of OC symptoms in varying proportions. We should tailor CBT for the OC symptoms of patients after the consideration of their verbal ability along with the improvement of their environmental conditions, such as moving them to a more suitable school/work place/habitat. Among these efforts, newly invented therapies, such as ST, should be tried in conjunction with CBT.

## Further Readings

Bejerot S. (2007). An autistic dimension: a proposed subtype of obsessive-compulsive disorder. *Autism, 11*, 101–110.

Thiel, N., Tuschen, B., Herbst, N., Külz, A., Nissen, C., Hertenstein, E., … Voderholzer, U. (2014). The prediction of treatment outcomes by early maladaptive schemas and schema modes in obsessive-compulsive disorder. *BMC Psychiatry, 14(1)*, 362.

Storch, E.A., Nadeau, J.M., Johnco, C., Timpano, K., McBride, N., Mutch, P.J., … Murphy, T.K. (2016). Hoarding in youth with autism spectrum disorders and anxiety: Incidence, clinical correlates, and behavioral treatment response. *Journal of Autism and Developmental Disorders,* [Epub, Advance online publication].

Chapter 36

# Innovations in cognitive behaviour therapy for the treatment of co-existing mental health and substance misuse

Hermine Graham and Amanda Baker

## Overview

Cognitive-behaviour therapy (CBT) has established itself as the evidence-based psychological treatment of choice for a range of mental health conditions, and is is recommended in national treatment and policy guidances. However, the research trials which form the underpinnings of this evidence base have often needed to exclude participants with comobidities, particularly drug or alcohol misuse, for the purpose of simplicity and purity. Thus many CBT recommended treatment protocols and manualised approaches for common and more severe mental health problems have not been developed with those who experience comorbid mental health and substance misuse problems in mind. However, prevalence studies across a range of countries consistently indicate that alcohol and drug misuse are very common in those with mental health problems. Co-existing mental health and substance use are associated with poor engagement in mental health treatment and poorer treatment outcomes. An epidemiologic study carried out in the USA found that 16.7% of adults will experience alcohol or drug problems in their lifetimes. In contrast, for those who experience anxiety and depression the prevalence rates are significantly higher; 32% will use substances problematically and the figure is 47% for those who experience schizophrenia. For young people rates are higher still.

## Major Findings

A number of countries, in recognition of the significant impact of comorbidity on treatment outcomes, have in recent years developed policy guidelines in an attempt to integrate the management and treatment of those with comorbid mental health and substance misuse problems. Nonetheless, protocol driven CBT for disorders such as anxiety, depression and psychosis continues to be routinely offered for single disorders and do not address co-existing substance misuse. Over the last two decades significant strides have been made in a number of countries including Australia, Canada, the United Kingdom (UK) and the United States (US) to develop treatments that integrate the treatment of co-exisiting mental health and substance misuse. Systematic reviews of this literature suggest that interventions that are brief and include CBT, family, motivational and behavioural elements are effective in the treatment of these comorbidities. However, due to methodological variations and limitations between studies there has not yet been conclusive evidence to indicate that one psychosocial treatment confers greater benefit than another in terms of reducing substance use or improving mental state for those with comorbidities.

Recommendations from the literature have been for the need to evaluate brief interventions, to enable service providers to identify a cost-effective and easy to implement component that can be quickly integrated into standard interventions. As a result there are a number of treatment trials that have recently sought to refine and develop innovative CBT approaches that include motivational elements to evaluate their effectiveness in treating common and severe mental health problems that co-exist with drug and alcohol problems. These trials have been conducted in a range of settings including psychiatric inpatient, community mental health and substance misuse, out-patient, social networking and on-line settings. The results of these studies are now emerging and showing promise. They indicate that including or integrating CBT interventions for substance misuse into treatments for mental health problems can lead to greater improvement in outcomes than interventions for mental health alone.

### Clinical Implications

CBT is now routinely offered for a number of mental health problems. However, if close to 50% of people who are offered CBT also have co-existing alcohol or drug problems then if it is ignored during treatment sessions this will have a negative impact upon treatment outcomes and trials that seek to establish the effectiveness of CBT. These recent studies that include or integrate CBT interventions for substance misuse into CBT treatments for mental health problems such as anxiety, depression and psychosis indicate that it may lead to improved outcomes. Clients benefit from the opportunity to consider the impact of their substance use on their mental health and become aware of the possibility that continued use may interact negatively with mental health thereby maintaining a vicious cycle of mental health and substance misuse problems.

## Future Directions

Integrating brief, easy to implement components for addressing substance use into standard CBT protocols and manuals for the range of mental health problems may optimise outcomes for CBT. Future research would benefit from large scale randomised controlled trials and identifying the specifc ingredients necessary to improve the outcomes of CBT for those with co-existing mental health and substance misuse problems. Specific ingredients worthy of further research include identifyng; the optimal length of such components, mechanisms or processes of change, whether it is more effective to include or integrate the component or a module within standard CBT protocols and which disorders and client groups experience most improvements when substance misuse is addressed routinely as part of the CBT they receive. Perhaps future trials of CBT would benefit from including such a component and those with co-existing alcohol and drug problems, rather than excluding them, to enable resultant treatment protocols and manuals to be generalisable.

## Further Readings

Baker, A., & Velleman, R. (Eds.). (2007). *Clinical handbook of co-existing mental health and drug and alcohol problems.* London, England: Routledge.

Graham H.L., Copello, A., Birchwood, M.J. & Mueser, K.T. (Eds.) (2003). *Substance misuse in psychosis: Approaches to treatment and service delivery.* Chichester, England: Wiley.

Hunt, G.E., Segfried, N., Morley, K., Sitharthian, T., Cleary, M. (2013). Psychosocial interventions for people with both severe mental illness and substance misuse. *Cochrane Database of Systematic Reviews.* doi: 10.1002/14651858.CD001088.pub3

Chapter 37

# How do we best treat comorbid substance use and mental disorders? Evidence-based approaches to integrated treatment

Mark Deady, Katherine Mills, Maree Teesson, Frances Kay-Lambkin, Joanne Ross, Andrew Baillie, and Mirjana Subotic

## Overview

Comorbidity of mental illness and substance use disorders is a significant challenge facing health systems globally. Historically, several models of treating comorbid mental health and substance use disorders (MHSUD) have been used, guided by different aetiological models of comorbidity. These include: 'sequential,' 'parallel,' 'integrated,' and 'stepped care' treatment approaches. Integrated treatments have intuitive appeal and present a number of advantages over other approaches. Treatment by a single service helps to ensure internally consistent treatment with common objectives that can explore the complex relationship between conditions. This single point of contact reduces burden on the individual, along with potential communication problems and discordant treatment philosophies, reducing the chance of clients 'falling through the gaps' when it comes to treatment. Over the last ten years much work has been done to further the evidence-base in this area. The synthesised evidence has found that integrated interventions in comorbid populations can be effective while translation and policy responses are also increasing. Unfortunately effectiveness trials of specific man-ualised therapies (phase 4 trials) are rare.

## Major Findings

Most evidence to support the use of integrated MHSUD treat-ment has been in the area of psychotic disorders, and in practice integrating across service settings has proven diffi-cult. Pharmacological interventions are a predominant form of treatment for psychotic spectrum disorders along with other disorders, although these treatments can form an important part of treatment, for the sake of this brevity these will not be discussed.

There is currently no good evidence regarding effectiveness of one psychosocial treatment over another for psychotic spectrum disorders comorbid with substance use disorders (SUDs). However, studies incorporating integrated psychoso-cial treatments have been showing promise. For instance, assertive community treatment — a structured, intensive approach to case-management of individuals with co-occur-ring SUDs and psychotic disorders which aims to enhance engagement, treatment, and retention—has been associated with improvements regarding substance use outcomes, quality of life, and hospitalisation.

In some cases of common mental disorders, many symptoms exhibited by individuals with SUDs will subside following a period of abstinence and stabilisation without the need for any direct attention. In other cases psychosocial and/or pharmacological interventions are required.

Historically, there have been over-restrictive attitudes towards pharmacological treatments for MHSUD due to propensity for abuse. However, considering the safety of most of the newer medications (e.g., selective serotonin reuptake inhibitors) such caution cannot be justified. Nevertheless, it is observed that psychological therapy should at least be an adjunct to pharmacotherapy, if not a first-line treatment strategy, for individuals with common mental disorders and co-occurring substance use. Recent reviews indicate integrated psychological treatment for SUDs and depressive or anxiety disorders is effective in reducing symptoms of both conditions, with longer interventions generally producing the best outcomes. Of the limited studies available, CBT techniques (particularly in combination with motivational interviewing) have good evidence of efficacy; with recent advances in the areas of eHealth, behavioural activation, and brief interventions showing significant promise. Research on psychological treatments for comorbid bipolar disorder and SUDs is scarce, however, recent evidence suggests integrating treatments for both disorders is effective.

Due to the interrelatedness of posttraumatic stress disorder (PTSD) and substance use, it is recommended that these conditions be treated in an integrated fashion. Psychotherapy is recommended as the first line treatment of adults with PTSD. The recently published COPE trial provides support for the use of prolonged exposure among individuals with PTSD and SUDs. Because exposure therapy can be anxiety inducing, it is recommended that the individual would have significantly reduced substance use and appropriate relapse prevention skills before exposure therapy is utilised, this is also true of this technique when applied to social phobia. Present-focused therapies have also been associated with clinically significant reductions in PTSD symptoms and substance use, although findings are often comparable to other therapies.

Research on psychological treatments for comorbid social anxiety and SUDs is scarce, and early studies of psychological treatments in this population proved ineffective, however, recent work integrating treatment for both disorders has had positive results. Currently, a large Australian randomised trial of integrated treatment for combined alcohol use and social phobia (CASP) is underway.

## Clinical Implications

Combinations of different therapeutic styles and modalities, such as various psychotherapies, pharmacotherapies, and behavioural treatments can often exert a synergistic effect on treatment, while time spent in treatment moderates improvement regardless of substance used. However, bringing all these elements together in a coherent and pragmatic manner continues to be a challenge to the field. Nevertheless, evidence suggests that if consistently applied, individuals in integrated treatment programmes achieve long-term positive recovery and stable outcomes across MHSUDs, as well as hospitalisation and homelessness, and improved social and emotional outcomes and quality of life.

## Future Directions

Further effectiveness trials of specific manualised therapies are required. Additionally, more clinical and translational research is required into the benefits of enhancing treatment approaches for comorbid problems via the use of technology. Ideally, integration should stretch toward a holistic health framework (including physical health) and also incorporate the broader social services system (housing, employment, etc.).

Finally, systemic issues in health care systems often limit dissemination and application of effective treatments. These challenges require a better, more sophisticated system of care that has the capacity to deliver integrated, coherent interventions in flexible modalities and across service settings. Publicly funded health care, including mental health care, has traditionally struggled to respond to an increasing demand for services in a context of limited financial, physical and, importantly, human resources.

## Future Readings

Mental Health and Drug Alcohol Office (2015). *Effective models of care for comorbid mental illness and illicit substance use: Evidence check review.* New South Wales, Australia: NSW Ministry of Health.

Mills K.L., Teesson M., Back S.E., Brady, K.T., Baker, A.L., Hopwood, S., ... Ewer, P.L. (2012). Integrated exposure-based therapy for co-occurring posttraumatic stress disorder and substance dependence: A randomized controlled. *JAMA, 308*(7), 690–699.

Chapter 38

# Outcome evaluation in a private practice setting

Chris Mackey and Megan L. Henderson

## Overview

Much outcome research in the cognitive-behaviour therapy (CBT) field focuses on treatment 'efficacy', based on highly selected participants within randomised controlled trial research designs. However, such findings might not be readily generalisable. Treatment 'effectiveness' studies, by contrast, are conducted within routine clinical practice, including private psychology settings. Such research provides arguably more relevant data for therapists, consumers and government funding bodies. There is little reported CBT effectiveness outcome research within the Australian literature.

This chapter aims to present effectiveness outcome data on over 2000 adult and adolescent clients seen for individual therapy based on CBT models from 2007 to mid-2015 at Chris Mackey and Associates, a private psychology practice in Geelong. All clients accessed sessions under the Medicare Better Access scheme, funded partly by federal government rebates and partly by client co-payments. Our results provide support for the clinical effectiveness of CBT interventions funded under this scheme. This research provides a solid benchmark for effectiveness research within real world settings in Australia and has clinical implications for relevant federal funding initiatives.

## Major Findings

Our most fundamental findings compared adult pre-treatment and post-treatment questionnaire scores on the Beck Anxiety Inventory (BAI) and Beck Depression Inventory (BDI). These data are currently available for 1,943 out of 3094 adult clients (62.8%) seen for a mean of 8.2 sessions ($SD$ = 7.2). Over 100 additional clients are yet to complete treatment. BAI mean scores reduced from 18.0 ($SD$ = 11.3) to 10.4 ($SD$ = 9.9), and BDI mean scores reduced from 19.7 ($SD$ = 9.9) to 10.7 ($SD$ = 9.7). Results are both clinically and statistically significant, representing an average reduction in anxiety and depressive symptoms from a mild-moderate level, well within the clinical range, to a slight-mild level, around the threshold between the normal and clinical range. These data translate into an effect size of 0.78 for the BAI and 0.97 for the BDI, meaning the average client at the end of treatment was better off than approximately 80% of clients at the start of treatment in terms of symptomatic distress.

We are also interested in client response to therapy for Major Depressive Disorder (MDD) with or without medication. At last count we had collected outcome data on 680 adult clients with MDD, representing approximately two thirds of our clients seen for this condition through the Medicare scheme. For the 384 clients treated with combined therapy and medication, their BDI mean scores reduced from 27.3 ($SD$ = 8.7) to 14.30 ($SD$ = 10.8), reducing from moderate to mild severity in an average of 10.2 sessions ($SD$ = 9.3). For the 282 clients with MDD who were not on medication, their BDI mean scores reduced from 25.9 ($SD$ = 8.2) to 13.0 ($SD$ = 10.7) in an average of 9.1 sessions ($SD$ = 7.3). Intermediate data collected at session 5 showed that they reported an equivalent degree and rate of recovery for both anxiety and depressive symptoms throughout treatment.

These data affirm our view that many people can be effectively treated for depression without medication, and support the emerging view that psychological therapy can often be a primary treatment intervention for MDD.

In response to initial criticism that the Medicare Better Access scheme mainly catered for adult clients, our research explored the clinical effectiveness of CBT for adolescents. In our practice, over 20% of those referred through the scheme are aged under 18 years. Of the 264 clients aged 13 to 17 years old from whom we sought to collect outcome data using the same measures, 129 completers (48.9% of sample) reported improvement comparable to that of adults. Mean adolescent BAI scores reduced from 18.9 ($SD$ = 11.2) to 11.7 ($SD$ = 10.1), and mean BDI scores reduced from 19.4 ($SD$ = 10.4) to 10.3 ($SD$ = 9.3), with an effect size of 0.71 on the BAI and 0.87 on the BDI.

Additional results on children aged from 10 to 17 years assessed by comparable Beck Youth measures are now available. We shall then additionally report on results using briefer measures for over 90% of all clients seen, as well as results using measures of positive wellbeing.

## Clinical Implications

The main findings endorse the effectiveness and efficiency of CBT interventions for a broad and representative range of clients seen in an everyday clinical setting. The similar treatment effects obtained for adult and adolescent clients across a range of measures of symptomatic distress suggest that the overall benefits of CBT are relatively robust, and generalisable across a broad age range.

CBT was found to be effective for significant mental health problems, specifically MDD. These findings support our anecdotal observations that many people can be effectively treated for depression without medication, and that psychological treatment can often be an effective primary treatment for MDD.

We believe that collecting outcome data and providing clients with timely feedback about their relative progress, in itself, can enhance therapy effectiveness.

**Future Directions**

This research shows that conducting routine clinical therapy evaluation is achievable in everyday settings. More outcome data of this type is needed with a diverse range of client groups from a wide range of mental health settings. This would help to further establish benchmarks for anticipated treatment effectiveness in real-world settings. Subsequent research could help identify predictors of response to therapy.

It seems noteworthy that our outcome evaluation findings have had some influence at a wider professional and political level, having been incorporated into official government and research reports on the Better Access scheme, and supporting ongoing funding for the scheme when it has been under threat.

We shall also continuously update our more detailed findings on the research page of our practice website (http://chrismackey.com.au/education/our-research).

## Further Readings

Pirkis, J., Ftanou, M., Williamson, M., Machlin, A., Spittal, M., Bassilios, B., & Harris, M. (2011). Australias Better Access initiative: An evaluation. *The Australian and New Zealand Journal of Psychiatry, 45 (9),* 726–739.

Section 11


Transdiagnostic Issues

Chapter 39

# The dread of death and its relationship to mental health

Rachel E. Menzies and Lisa Iverach

## Overview

Death anxiety has featured in art, literature, song, myth and cultural rituals throughout human history. In both ancient and modern societies, death has been personified in various forms, such as a grim reaper stalking the terrified living. This brief chapter will explore the argument that the dread of death may underpin a range of mental health disorders. The major theory within social psychology that explores death anxiety and its impact, namely Terror Management Theory (TMT), will also be introduced.

## Major Findings

The human understanding of death is clearly not present from birth, and the nature and progression of death fears has been the subject of much developmental research. Various components of this understanding, such as the inevitability and irreversibility of death, appear to be mastered by children in stages. Notably, the growth in this awareness of mortality appears to coincide with a rise in anxiety and phobic reactions, suggesting that a relationship between fears of death and mental health issues may be present by 7 or 8 years of age. The first anxiety disorder to emerge in terms of age of onset — separation anxiety disorder — appears to explicitly relate to death anxiety. Separation anxiety disorder involves persistent worry about losing major attachment figures, or the self, through misadventure during separation. The condition often involves nightmares and rumination with death themes.

Several other lines of research support the notion that death fears underlie many mental health problems. Most of this research has been conducted with adult patients. First, patient verbal reports strongly suggest a role for death anxiety in psychiatric disorders. Many individuals with illness anxiety disorder and somatoform disorders report that body scanning, palpating of lymph nodes, and requests for repeated medical tests, are the result of a desperate desire to stay alive. Similarly, those with panic disorder frequently state that fears of sudden heart attack drive their attendance at emergency services and repeated consultations with cardiologists. Most adults with agoraphobia report that avoidance of unfamiliar places and refusal to travel without security figures is intended to prevent harm from sudden misadventure or collapse. Further, it has been widely noted that the majority, if not all, of the specific phobias are associated with objects or situations that could result in death (e.g., heights, snakes, spiders, blood, water). Finally, most forms of obsessive-compulsive disorder (OCD) can be readily related to death. Compulsive washers typically associate their avoidance of bodily fluids, toxins and poisons with death to the self or loved ones. Similarly, compulsive checkers may repeatedly inspect power points, gas and electric cooktops, heaters, and door and window locks in a reported attempt to prevent fire, electrocution and home invasion. Even among OCD sufferers with pure obsessions, in which behavioural manifestations such as washing or checking are largely absent, themes of death are common. Some individuals with aggressive obsessions fear that they may inadvertently, in an altered state of awareness, take their own life (e.g., by walking into traffic) or the life of a loved one (e.g., by pushing someone in front of a train). Some patients appear to fear that their intrusive 'death' thoughts could magically cause the death of loved ones. Such individuals may use any means, including superstitious tapping, blinking or counting rituals to prevent death.

A second line of evidence comes from experimental studies in OCD. The results of a series of laboratory studies on compulsive washing are consistent with the verbal reports of OCD sufferers described above. Compared to age- and sex-matched non-OCD controls, OCD participants have been shown to have higher 'death threat' expectancies in contamination paradigms. In addition, high positive correlations have been found between the expectation of death in these studies and various aspects of OCD symptomatology (e.g., anxiety scores in the task, urge to wash ratings, and time spent washing after the task). Further, when death expectancy has been experimentally manipulated through instruction, high expectancy conditions have been found to increase anxiety and escape behaviours.

A third line of evidence comes from experimental studies using the mortality salience (MS) paradigm emerging from TMT. TMT proposes that the desire to stay alive, coupled with the knowledge that one's death can occur at any moment, has the power to produce crippling fear. MS studies explore this possibility by priming individuals in the laboratory with subtle cues of death before assessing the impact of these primes on subsequent behaviour. Among other findings in this large and growing field of enquiry, mortality salience priming has been shown to increase anxiety-related behaviours in specific phobias, social phobia, and OCD.

Finally, recent findings provide evidence of positive correlations between scores on death anxiety scales and number of mental health diagnoses, severity of illness ratings, number of hospitalisations and severity of mental health problems. Though the causal nature of these associations is yet to be established, the strong relationships are at least consistent with the suggestion that death fears may mediate mental health problems.

### Clinical Implications

If the dread of death is a mediator of mental health disorders, treatment approaches that explicitly address these existential fears may be necessary. Conventional treatments that fail to target death anxiety may result in a 'revolving door' of individuals presenting with a shifting array of mental illnesses across their lifespan. Therapeutic approaches that may prove efficacious include existential psychotherapy, acceptance and commitment therapy (ACT) and cognitive-behaviour therapy (CBT). Conventional treatments may also benefit from various approaches to end of life care, including dignity therapy, meaning-centred therapy, and cognitive existential group therapy. Such treatment perspectives often focus on accepting the inevitability of death, and using this acceptance to build a meaningful life centred on the individual's core values.

### Future Directions

Several different research questions and directions arise from the extant data. First, as suggested above, there is a need to clarify the nature of the relationship between death fears and mental health status. Second, what is the longer term impact of MS priming on anxiety-related behaviour? To date, laboratory studies have focused only on the first hour after priming. Third, what are the optimal components of treatment programs targeting death fears? Treating the dread of death is in its infancy within CBT, but has a longer tradition within other brands of therapy (e.g., existential psychotherapy). Finally, does explicitly targeting death fears in treatment produce better long-term outcomes? If the dread of death is the 'worm at the core' of the human psyche, it may prove very hard to shift.

## Further Readings

Iverach, L., Menzies, R.G., & Menzies, R.E. (2014). Death anxiety and its role in psychopathology: Reviewing the status of a transdiagnostic construct. *Clinical Psychology Review, 34,* 580–593.

Menzies, R.G., Menzies, R.E., & Iverach, L. (2015). The role of death fears in obsessive-compulsive disorder. *Australian Clinical Psychologist, 1,* 6–11.

Yalom, I.D. (2008). *Staring at the Sun: Overcoming the terror of death.* San Francisco, CA: Jossey-Bass.

Chapter 40

# New approaches in theory and treatment of clinical perfectionism in social anxiety, obsessive-compulsive disorder and eating disorders

Sarah Egan

## Overview

Clinical perfectionism involves striving to meet high personal standards despite negative consequences and basing self-worth on attainment of standards. Perfectionism is elevated in numerous psychological disorders. Perfectionism has been noted as a risk and maintaining factor for a range of disorders including depression, social anxiety, obsessive-compulsive disorder (OCD), and eating disorders. Perfectionism has also been found to predict poorer outcome in cognitive-behaviour therapy (CBT) for social anxiety, depression, and OCD. Furthermore, perfectionism is associated with higher comorbidity. Given this evidence we have proposed that perfectionism is a transdiagnostic process, and that treating it should lead to reductions in a range of psychopathologies. There is evidence from a number of studies that CBT for perfectionism leads to a reduction in a range of symptoms of psychopathology, including anxiety, depression, social anxiety, obsessive-compulsive symptoms, and eating disorders. Research in clinical perfectionism is focusing not only on treatment studies, but also understanding the mechanisms involved in the maintenance of perfectionism through testing theoretical models of the construct, and also on prevention.

## Major Findings

Current research in clinical perfectionism is examining a number of areas to improve the theoretical understanding and treatment of perfectionism. The cognitive behavioural model of clinical perfectionism that was introduced by Shafran and colleagues has guided the development of CBT for perfectionism. The model involves cognitive and behavioural factors that maintain clinical perfectionism, including for example, setting rigid standards for performance, self-criticism over not meeting standards, and re-setting of standards higher even when a standard is successfully met. One of the important aspects that was outlined in the original model was the role of cognitive and interpretation biases through which the individual judges their performance, including selective attention towards failure related information and discounting of success. In a recent study by Howell et al., we aimed to examine the hypothesis from this model, that individuals with clinical perfectionism have an attentional bias towards negative information compared to positive information, when it is perfectionism relevant. Using an experimental design with an attentional probe task, we found that high perfectionists, in comparison to low perfectionists, had an attentional bias towards negative rather than positive information, but only for perfectionism relevant information. These results support the hypotheses of Shafran and colleagues' model of clinical perfectionism. These developments may help to refine

CBT for perfectionism and inform understanding of the processes through which CBT for perfectionism impacts on a range of psychological symptoms.

In the model of clinical perfectionism, one of the key aspects is self-worth being based predominately on striving and achievement, i.e., the over-evaluation of self-worth on achievement. In CBT for perfectionism, this is one of the key components that the clinician aims to address, as it is from this dysfunctional scheme for self-evaluation that the other maintaining processes in the model come from, hence the importance of understanding this component further. Frost and colleagues have conducted a program of research examining contingent self-worth in perfectionism. The concept of contingent self-worth is similar to the idea of over-evaluation of striving and achievement in the cognitive-behavioural model of clinical perfectionism. At the heart of this is the idea that if an individual bases their self-worth on achievement of standards, then they will experience a range of negative consequences, including low mood and anxiety, in addition to self-criticism when they inevitably fail to meet these standards. Frost et al. have conducted recent research examining contingent self-worth and found it is a risk factor for OCD. Furthermore, they have concluded that contingent self-worth along with constructs such as self-ambivalence is important to include in cognitive-behavioural models of OCD.

Current research by our group is also focusing on the role of perfectionism in OCD and how to improve outcomes for those people with OCD who have elevated perfectionism. The role of perfectionism has long been recognised in OCD, and is one of the key cognitive constructs put forward by the Obsessive Compulsive Cognitions Working Group (OCCWG). There have been many studies showing perfectionism is elevated in individuals with OCD, and that it predicts poorer treatment response in individual and group CBT for OCD. This has led to the question, is CBT for perfectionism an effective intervention for OCD? Our pilot study has shown that CBT for perfectionism results in significant reductions in OCD, and improvements in quality of life.

Another recent development has been a focus on intervention for perfectionism as a target for prevention of mental health disorders. One line of research is examining if intervention for perfectionism can prevent eating disorders. Interventions for perfectionism have promise given many studies have implicated perfectionism as a risk and maintenance factor for eating disorders. In recent work by our research group we have investigated the efficacy of an online program for clinical perfectionism to examine if this can reduce the onset of eating disorders and associated anxiety and depression, in female adolescents and young adults. This research may be useful as a way to effectively disseminate prevention given the program is online.

### Clinical Implications

Research in CBT for clinical perfectionism has several implications, for targeting perfectionism directly in clients with elevated perfectionism who do not respond to standard CBT interventions, and as prevention for the development of psychological disorders.

### Future Directions

The findings regarding selective attention suggest future research should assess the causal role of attentional bias in clinical perfectionism and Attention Bias Modification techniques. Furthermore, research should examine mechanisms of change in CBT for perfectionism, for example, by determining if selective attention mediates change in perfectionism. Future research investigating contingent self-worth may help further understanding of the role of perfectionism in OCD. Research is also required which compares CBT for perfectionism to gold standard treatments for OCD, such as exposure and response prevention. Studies should also explore if CBT for perfectionism can improve outcomes and reduce relapse in OCD. Similar research is needed in social anxiety, where perfectionism also predicts poorer outcome to CBT. Finally, there is potential in future research examining perfectionism as a prevention program for a wide range of disorders.

## Further Readings

Egan, S.J., Wade, T.D., & Shafran, R. (2011). Perfectionism as a transdiagnostic process: A clinical review. *Clinical Psychology Review, 31,* 203–212.

Egan, S.J., Wade, T.D., Shafran, R., & Antony, M.M. (2014). *Cognitive-behavioral treatment of perfectionism.* New York, NY: Guilford.

Howell, J., McEvoy, P.M., Grafton, B., MacLeod, C., Kane, R.T., Anderson, R.A., & Egan, S.J. (2016). Selective attention in perfectionism: Dissociating valence from perfectionism-relevance. *Journal of Behavior Therapy and Experimental Psychiatry, 51,*100–108.

Chapter 41

# When fear and sadness turn into pathological emotions: The transdiagnostic process of generalisation

Kim Haesen, Jens Van Lier, Peter Lovibond, and Ann Meulders

## Overview

In order to assess unfamiliar situations, we extrapolate from our experiences with similar situations. For example, sunny days might remind you of a painful sunburn you experienced in the past and motivate you to wear sunblock. Emotions and cognitions generalise across similar contexts shaping our behaviour and facilitating adaptive coping with environmental demands. However, excessive generalisation can result in maladaptive behaviours, including emotional disorders. For example, depressed patients think of themselves as failures in every aspect of life. Patients suffering from posttraumatic stress disorder (PTSD) show anxiety in a variety of situations that remind them of the traumatic event. Chronic pain patients believe all movements will cause or exacerbate pain. These negative emotions trigger avoidance responses in a large variety of situations that in turn can have extremely disabling effects on the everyday functioning of patients. Moreover, intense emotional responses to numerous safe occasions may result in depletion of cognitive resources and hyperactivation of brain regions involved in the fear-learning networks, resulting in chronic anxiety.

In this chapter we discuss different forms of generalisation and their underlying mechanisms; for example, inductive reasoning, conceptual generalisation and processing styles.

## Major Findings

A single traumatic experience often suffices to produce fear learning about the context in which the trauma took place. Because a context is typically a complex constellation of stimuli, a selection mechanism is needed to restrict fear to the most likely predictors of harm in that context and to prevent fear from overgeneralising to a broad range of redundant stimuli. This selection mechanism ensures that fear only generalises to situations that accurately predict danger. In the case of PTSD, however, fear symptoms typically lack this restriction and generalise widely across redundant stimuli. For example, a car-accident victim might experience intense panic attacks when confronted with red lights that remind her of the traffic lights at the scene of the accident. Fear generalisation research has mainly focused on generalisation of conditioned fear reactions across simple stimuli that gradually differ from each other. Here, we introduce an alternative procedure in which a configuration of stimuli is paired with an electrical shock. Subsequent conditioned responding to part of the stimulus configuration is an indication of the level of stimulus selective fear learning.

Fear not only generalises to external cues or contexts, but to cues emerging from within the body as well. For example, a painful movement will elicit fear of movement-related pain through associative processes. In pain patients this fear spreads beyond movements or activities that were associated with pain during the original pain episode. One mechanism for this spreading of fear is stimulus generalisation based on perceptual similarity of proprioceptive stimuli. Fear of movement-related pain will be higher for movements that are highly similar to the originally painful movement. However, humans unlike other animals possess the capacity to abstract conceptual details of a learning episode, which allows them to generalise conditioned fear to physically dissimilar stimuli. In a Voluntary Movement Joystick paradigm participants learned that one type of action (moving the joystick to open boxes) was followed by pain, while another type of actions (closing boxes) was not. Fear of movement generalised to novel exemplars of the category 'opening boxes' but not to novel exemplars of the category 'closing boxes'.

These results suggest that generalisation of associative learning can also be seen as a form of inductive reasoning. The learner needs to infer rules during fear conditioning that help him decide how far to extrapolate this learning when faced with related but different stimuli. Fear conditioning research in which participants reported rules they adopted, has shown that humans show idiosyncratic rule induction and that the rules they induce determine the extent and shape of generalisation. However, high trait anxious participants who failed to learn a clear rule did not necessarily demonstrate excessive generalisation. These participants did show exaggerated shock expectancy in general.

Another mechanism underlying this excessive generalisation that has been studied is the way that individuals process negative and positive events. Individuals may think about the meanings, causes and implications of the event (i.e., abstract — 'why' thinking) or they may think about more perceptual concrete aspects of their event (i.e., concrete — 'how' thinking). This ruminative abstract processing style, often seen in depressed patients, might act as an important pathway towards excessive generalisation. Research using a depression-relevant conditioning paradigm while experimentally inducing participants in an abstract processing style has shown that this abstract processing style increased negative generalisation compared to a concrete processing style. These studies have shown that abstract thoughts can lead to over-generalisation of bad/failure feelings toward the self that is often seen in social anxiety and depression.

## Clinical Implications

Excessive generalisation is a core characteristic of individuals that suffer from emotional disorders (e.g., depression, anxiety disorders and chronic pain). Therefore, excessive generalisation may be considered a transdiagnostic marker for psychopathology. Understanding the mechanisms underlying generalisation provides opportunities for optimising treatments for emotional disorders. Stimulus-selective conditioning, rule learning and flexibility to switch to concrete processing styles are putative mechanisms that are receiving increasing interest in contemporary research.

## Future Directions

The presented data were all collected in healthy participants. To extend these findings to clinical populations future research comparing clinical and healthy samples is required. Understanding the mechanisms of generalisation is a stepping-stone to treatments of emotional disorders. The next step is to investigate how the cost-benefit balance of generalisation can be restored and how to translate these findings to treatment programs that can be implemented in clinical practice.

## Further Readings

Meulders, A., Vandael, K., & Vlaeyen, J.W.S. (under review). Generalization of pain-related fear based on conceptual knowledge. *Behavior Therapy.*

Van Lier, J., Vervliet, B., Vanbrabant, K., Lenaert, B., Raes, F. (2014). Abstract thinking about negative events in dysphoric students leads to negative generalization. *Journal of Experimental Psychopathology, 5,* 314–328.

Chapter 42

# Interventions for transdiagnostic processes in emotional disorders

Junwen Chen, Kristy Johnstone, Shin-ichi Ishikawa, Peter M. McEvoy, Alexander Tee, David Rimmington, Kirsten Vale, Rachel Graville, Sarra Hayes, Robert Kane, Jonathan Foster, and Jennifer Hudson

## Overview

Anxiety and depression account for more than half of the burden of disease caused by mental disorders. Anxiety and depression also co-occur highly with each other, with 69% of anxious individuals being diagnosed with depression and up to 75% of depressed individuals meeting criteria for an anxiety disorder. When different classes of disorders co-occur at such high rates, selecting an appropriate treatment approach can be challenging. Unlike most traditional disorder-specific treatments, transdiagnostic approaches target common features underlying symptoms in comorbid disorders. They are more time-efficient and cost effective, simplifying treatment for both the client and therapist, which could improve the quality of care and satisfy a great need in public health. This chapter focuses on interventions for trans-diagnostic processes in emotional disorders. We reported results on underlying mechanisms involving transdiagnostic processes, and intervention strategies targeting transdiagnostic processes in populations with anxiety and depression.

## Major Findings

To investigate the mechanism underlying cognitive variables across childhood anxiety symptoms, we proposed a cognitive behavioural model involving cognitive errors and negative self-statements that may contribute to six childhood anxiety symptoms. Participants were community children ($n$ = 532), adolescents ($n$ = 751), and youth with anxiety disorders ($n$ = 41), who completed the Spence Children's Anxiety Scale, the Children's Self-Statement Scale, and the Children's Cognitive Error Scale. Multiple group analysis revealed that unconstrained model demonstrated better fit than the constrained models, suggesting heterogeneity among the groups. Furthermore, the mediating effect of negative self-statements on the relationship between cognitive errors and childhood anxiety was supported in the community but not the other populations.

Recent research has proposed that excessive worry, a repeated cognitive process concerning potential negative events, is a transdiagnostic process across anxiety and depression. Worry functions as cognitive avoidance that prevents emotional processing of fear in anxiety and also increases depressive symptoms through activating negative feelings about an upcoming event. This disrupts the implementation of effective problem solving strategies, resulting in maintained or exacerbated distress. Therefore, training in the skill of mindfulness (i.e., purposely devoting attention in the present moment in a non-evaluative way), Behavioural Activation (BA; i.e., reduce avoidance by activating functional, goal-oriented behaviour), and Self-compassion (SC; i.e., reduce avoidance by accepting negative experiences or situations) may help to break this vicious cycle of worry.

To address this issue, we investigated the efficacy of a mindfulness and acceptance-based group therapy (MABGT) for excessive worry by comparing it with a waitlist control (WLC). Fourteen participants from the community were randomised to either the MABGT condition, whereby they received eight 2-hour weekly treatment sessions, or the WLC. Results revealed a significant time effect for worry, with a large within-group effect size for pre to post-treatment in the MABGT condition but a small effect in the WLC. Compared to the WLC, the MABGT condition showed significant reduction in scores of Intolerance of Uncertainty from pre-treatment to post-treatment. The between-group effect size was moderate. Although both conditions produced a significant reduction in stress across time, the between-group effect size for stress at post-treatment was large.

Our further study focused on academic worry, a specific domain of general worry that is pervasively experienced among students. We examined (1) the relationship between academic worry and experiential avoidance (EA; i.e., a tendency to engage in avoidance); and (2) the effectiveness of BA and SC for reducing academic worry and EA compared to an active control of free writing. Participants were 83 students with moderate levels of academic worry. There was no significant correlation between trait EA and trait academic worry. However, all groups showed a significant decrease in distress about academic worry and general worry (all with large effect sizes). The BA and SC groups also showed a significant decrease in EA (BA: $d = .55$; SC: $d = .97$), while the control group showed no significant effect on EA ($d = .03$).

The search for unified transdiagnostic mechanisms of change can be extended to 'trans-therapy' mechanisms of change. To explore unified transdiagnostic mechanisms of change, we compared two techniques from different theoretical frameworks, namely attention training (ATT) and mindfulness-based progressive muscle relaxation (MB-PMR); both of which are designed to reduce anxiety by manipulating attention. While ATT reduces self-focused attention by encouraging individuals to attend to external auditory stimuli, MB-PMR requires individuals to attend internally to physical sensations in the present moment non-judgementally. Eighty-one participants with high trait anxiety were randomised to ATT, MB-PRM or a thought wandering (TW) control. We examined whether, compared to controls, both ATT and MB-PMR would impact state anxiety, and whether they would similarly or differentially influence several theory-driven mediators (change in negative metacognitive beliefs, present-focused attention, cognitive flexibility, and distancing). Results revealed that both active interventions, but not the control, showed a reduction in state anxiety and negative metacognitive beliefs, and an increase in distancing and present-focused attention.

## Clinical Implications

Overall, our results suggest the importance of anxious cognitions as potential transdiagnostic factors across childhood anxiety symptoms, which should be emphasised and tested in future transdiagnostic approaches for youth. To target excessive worry as a transdiagnostic process, training in the skill of mindfulness and acceptance, and behavioural activation may be effective in improving worry, and worry-related cognitions and distress. Furthermore, it is possible that the mechanisms of change across different interventions are more similar than different. Hence, identifying trans-therapy factors may help to determine the most critical treatment focus to achieve successful treatment outcomes.

## Future Directions

Future research should take into account the commonalities and differences across clinical and non-clinical populations in regard to cognitive factors as transdiagnostic processes across anxiety symptoms. Studies should also replicate and verify our preliminary findings with a larger sample and further investigate the mechanisms underlying the changes via transdiagnostic approaches. Furthermore, regardless of the specific treatment model from which they derive, evaluating the most powerful and efficient techniques for modifying mechanisms that maintain the symptoms is warranted.

## Further Readings

Ehrenreich-May, J., & Chu, B. C. (Eds.). (2013). *Transdiagnostic treatments for children and adolescents: principles and practice.* New York, NY: Guilford.

Norton, P. J., & Paulus, D. J. (2015). Toward a unified treatment for emotional disorders: update on the science and practice. *Behavior Therapy.* doi:10.1016/j.beth.2015.07.002

Chapter 43

# Innovations in transdiagnostic internet and face-to-face treatments for anxiety and depression in adults

Jill M. Newby

## Overview

Until recently, disorder-specific treatments — where separate cognitive-behaviour therapy (CBT) protocols targeted separate disorders — has dominated the way we treat depression and anxiety. While this approach is effective, there are also drawbacks: the ever-growing number of manuals is a barrier to dissemination and training; these interventions pay limited attention to comorbidity; there are limitations to the reliability and validity of the diagnoses that these protocols are based on; and there are more similarities than differences in the factors that cause and maintain depression and anxiety. Driven by these concerns there has been a relatively recent 'paradigm shift' in the treatment literature, with a shift away from the disorder-specific approach in favour of a transdiagnostic approach to conceptualisation and treatment of these disorders. Transdiagnostic treatments are theory-driven, aiming to target the core maintaining processes across presenting issues, and provide a pragmatic and efficient way to address multiple comorbidities and problems. The transdiagnostic treatments that have been evaluated tend to fall into two broad approaches: traditional CBT interventions, and third-wave mindfulness-based and acceptance-based approaches. Both approaches have demonstrated to be effective, and provide empirically supported treatment options for individuals with depression and/or anxiety.

## Major Findings

Both randomised controlled trials (RCTs) and effectiveness studies in routine clinical practice show that transdiagnostic treatments for anxiety and depression, or mixed anxiety disorders, lead to large and significant reductions in depression, anxiety, disability and distress. They outperform control groups, including usual care, waiting list, and active psychological treatment controls, although they have never been compared to antidepressant medications. Preliminary evidence suggests that transdiagnostic CBT appears to be at least equally effective to the disorder-specific CBT, but may yield small but superior effects compared to disorder-specific interventions in reducing depression symptoms (although it is unclear whether these differences are clinically significant).

Recent research shows that transdiagnostic interventions can be successfully delivered over the internet or via the computer at a fraction of clinical time, and therefore at a lower cost. However, receiving guidance and support from a trained clinician is critically important when clients participate in internet CBT to encourage adherence, and therefore, maximise outcomes. Transdiagnostic CBT interventions have been most widely evaluated out of the treatment modalities, although notably, recent research has started to explore the value of short-term transdiagnostic psychodynamic treatments. Transdiagnostic computerised, internet, group-based, and individual therapies have been now evaluated, with the Unified Protocol from Barlow and colleagues in the United States (US), and transdiagnostic group-based CBT for anxiety disorders developed by Norton and colleagues in the US and Australia being the most rigorously evaluated to-date.

We recently conducted a meta-analysis published in *Clinical Psychology Review* and found that the largest effect sizes were observed for computerised and individual interventions, with slightly smaller within-group reductions in depression and anxiety symptoms for group-based therapy. However, there have been no head-to-head comparisons between internet, group or individual transdiagnostic interventions, leaving an important direction for future research. The results of one clinical trial failed to find a difference between mindfulness based stress reduction and CBT for anxiety, and in another trial there were no differences between acceptance and commitment therapy and CBT for anxiety, likely due to a lack of power. On a larger scale, when the results were pooled across studies, we found some evidence in our meta-analysis showing that CBT resulted in slightly greater reductions in anxiety than mindfulness and acceptance-approaches, but there were no differences in reductions in depression. Future efforts need to be placed on identifying for whom CBT versus mindfulness and acceptance approaches work best, and how these interventions work. Interestingly, recent research on the Unified Protocol has revealed important information about the cognitive and emotional mechanisms of change during transdiagnostic emotion-focused therapy, including the role of reduced reactivity to negative emotions, in facilitating change.

## Clinical Implications

The results from clinical trials show that transdiagnostic computerised, internet-delivered and face-to-face treatments present an effective approach for the treatment of anxiety and depression across the lifespan. Although the evidence supporting these interventions is relatively new, this will not be new to clinicians who likely already implement a transdiagnostic approach to treatment in their clinical practice. There is a substantial body of evidence supporting the use of internet-delivered transdiagnostic CBT interventions in the treatment of depression and anxiety, particularly for adults. These interventions have the potential for widespread use, and optimise both treatment coverage, and have potential to increase access to evidence-based treatments for people who may not otherwise be able to access effective and affordable treatment. Internet-delivered CBT should be offered as routine treatment for individuals with anxiety and depressive disorders, as either stand-alone intervention, or blended with face-to-face treatment sessions.

## Future Directions

The dissemination of transdiagnostic interventions is the critical next step, and technology (e.g., apps) will help us achieve this. Future research should focus on unanswered key questions, including how transdiagnostic CBT compares to pharmacotherapy, whether combining CBT and other therapeutic approaches (e.g., mindfulness) enhances patient outcomes and reduces relapse, and the long-term effects of transdiagnostic interventions. Conducting RCTs of transdiagnostic interventions via the internet will enable us to determine the optimal ordering of treatment techniques to maximise treatment efficiency, to explore whether tailored or personalised interventions based on case formulation achieve better outcomes than fixed manualised interventions, and how mindfulness-based approaches compare to CBT. In addition, our team are currently evaluating a modular individualised transdiagnostic intervention designed to target the key transdiagnostic cognitive and behavioural variables that maintain symptoms (e.g., rumination/worry, intrusive memories). The results of this trial will reveal the acceptability and efficacy of modularised flexible approach to transdiagnostic treatment of emotional disorders.

## Further Readings

Newby, J.M., Mckinnon, A., Kuyken, W., Gilbody, S., & Dalgleish, T. (2015). Systematic review and meta-analysis of transdiagnostic psychological treatments for anxiety and depressive disorders in adulthood. *Clinical Psychology Review, 40*(0), 91–110. doi: http://dx.doi.org/10.1016/j.cpr.2015.06.002

Barlow, D.H., Allen, L.B., & Choate, M.L. (2004). Toward a unified treatment for emotional disorders. *Behavior Therapy, 35*(2), 205–230. doi: http://dx.doi.org/10.1016/S0005-7894(04)80036-4

Nordgren, L.B., Hedman, E., Etienne, J., Bodin, J., Kadowaki, Å., Eriksson, S., … Carlbring, P. (2014). Effectiveness and cost-effectiveness of individually tailored Internet-delivered cognitive behavior therapy for anxiety disorders in a primary care population: A randomized controlled trial. *Behaviour Research and Therapy, 59*(0), 1–11. doi: http://dx.doi.org/10.1016/j.brat.2014.05.00

Chapter 44

# Theoretical relevance of attentional bias, and starting point for treatment: The case of body dissatisfaction

Nienke C. Jonker and Peter J. de Jong

## Overview

Selective visual processing of disorder-relevant information (i.e., attentional bias) has been proposed to be a core characteristic of many psychiatric disorders. It has been shown to be involved in addiction, depression, eating disorders, and anxiety. For example, substance dependent individuals have been found to show an attentional bias for substance cues and people with post-traumatic stress disorder for trauma reminders. Current views suggest that it might be relevant to conceptualise psychopathology in terms of dysfunctional transdiagnostic processes instead of assuming a latent pathogenic factor. This sparked research expanding the traditional focus on disorder-specific biases to also cover biased attentional processing involved in dysfunctional transdiagnostic processes such as perfectionism, rumination, and body-dissatisfaction. In this chapter we will highlight some of the findings related to body-dissatisfaction that emerged from this transdiagnostic approach, discuss the potential clinical implications, and provide some directions for future research.

## Major Findings

Body dissatisfaction is associated with rumination, emotional distress and depression, and it is considered a key factor in the development, maintenance and relapse of eating disorders. Selective attention towards 'ugly' versus 'beautiful' body parts may well contribute to people's body dissatisfaction. As a first step to test the role of attentional bias in body dissatisfaction, eye movements of women with and women without body dissatisfaction were tracked, when they were looking at images of their body. Importantly, results indicated that specifically women who were dissatisfied with their body showed an attentional preference for body parts that they rated as relatively 'ugly'. As a second step the causal relation between such an attentional bias for 'ugly' body parts and body dissatisfaction needs to be examined. One way to test the proposed causal influence is to manipulate people's attentional bias and examine the effect on body dissatisfaction. An experimental study indeed showed that women who were trained to attend to their self-defined ugly body parts, showed a significant increase in body dissatisfaction. This shows that an attentional bias for ugly body parts can indeed play a role in the development of body dissatisfaction.

## Clinical Implications

The findings indicating that an attentional bias for ugly body parts is indeed involved in body dissatisfaction, together with research showing that inducing an attentional bias to ugly body parts increased women's dissatisfaction with their body, provide an important starting point for potential treatments. As such, mirror exposure has been proposed as an intervention for body dissatisfaction since it directly targets the way individuals look at their body. Recent work testing the efficacy of mirror exposure indeed showed that this treatment was very effective in improving participants' body satisfaction. However, in spite of its efficacy to improve body satisfaction, mirror exposure was not successful in systematically changing participants' viewing pattern. Therefore, complementary interventions that are successful in modifying participants' viewing pattern might provide additional benefit to individuals who are dissatisfied with their body. One class of interventions that has been designed to directly target individuals' attention is attention bias modification (ABM) training. Recent research using ABM as a means to train individuals to selectively attend to their own beautiful body parts showed that such ABM intervention can indeed successfully increase people's body satisfaction. Since training individuals to selectively attend to their ugly body parts was found to decrease their body satisfaction, the efficacy of ABM might be further enhanced by not only training to direct attention towards 'beautiful' body parts but also to train people to disengage attention from ugly body parts.

**Future Directions**

It would be important for future research to test whether indeed combining ABM with mirror exposure has added value in increasing body satisfaction and reducing eating disorder symptomatology. In addition, it would be relevant to test the role of attentional bias to cues related to other transdiagnostic processes such as rumination and perfectionism, or general traits such as reward and punishment sensitivity, and to explore whether modification of these attentional biases has clinical value.

## Further Readings

Smeets, E., Jansen, A., & Roefs, A. (2011). Bias for the (un) attractive self: On the role of attention in causing body (dis)satisfaction. *Health Psychology, 30,* 360–367.

van Hemel-Ruiter, M.E., de Jong, P.J., Oldehinkel, A.J., & Ostafin, B.D. (2013). Reward-related attentional biases and adolescent substance use. *Psychology of Addictive Behaviors, 27,* 142–150.

Verwoerd, J., Wessel, I., & de Jong P.J. (2012). Fewer intrusions after an attentional bias modification training for perceptual reminders of analogue trauma. *Cognition and Emotion, 26,* 153–165.

# Section 12

# E-therapy

Chapter 45

# A recommended process for development and evaluation of eTools for mental health and wellbeing

Stoyan Stoyanov, Leanne Hides, David J. Kavanagh, Davina Sanders, Wendell Cockshaw, and Madhavan Mani

## Overview

Web or mobile application based interventions for mental health and wellbeing (hereafter 'eTools') have proliferated with the uptake of smartphones. This makes it difficult for potential users to select high quality tools to address their needs. Cognitive-behaviour therapists face similar challenges when attempting to select and recommend eTools to their clients. Robust approaches to the development and evaluation of eTools are required to address these issues. The inclusion of potential users throughout the development process optimises the acceptability, utility and perceived relevance of eTools. Subsequent testing of eTools in randomised controlled trials (RCTs) is highly desirable. However, extended delays in the release and marketing of an eTool may mean it is superseded due to technological advancements or the release of similar eTools. When the results of RCTs are not yet available, minimum requirements comprise evidence-based content and uncontrolled outcome evaluations. Reporting of adherence to development processes such as these would offer a sound basis for eTool selection by practitioners and other users.

## Major Findings

Etools provide unprecedented opportunities for dissemination of real time cognitive-behaviour therapy (CBT) interventions for self-management of symptoms, or to supplement face-to-face treatments. However, selecting acceptable and impactful eTools is difficult for both the public and health practitioners alike, given the lack of consensus on this selection process. This chapter outlines an empirically sound approach to eTool development and evaluation that has been applied to the development of several web programs and mobile applications (apps) by the authors. The process has seven phases: contextual review, eTools review, participatory design workshops, expert concept design, iterative design and development, user testing, and outcome evaluation.

A preparatory phase of eTool development should incorporate a contextual review of current eTools in the proposed content area. A process similar to a systematic literature review should be adopted. This is easier said than done, as there is no database specifically dedicated to eHealth resources. For example, a search within the Apple App Store returns many irrelevant results, and omits quality resources of low popularity. Google searches may appear overwhelmingly large, but familiarisation with advanced search features can assist. For example the 'apps' filter in Google, used in conjunction with exclusion operators for irrelevant terms (e.g., NOT stress is currently searched as –stress) efficiently reduces the number of results. Thereafter, PRISMA flow guidelines for systematic literature reviews can be adopted. However,

Google's customisation of searches for user accounts and locations inhibits replicability of searches. This limitation may lead to omission of important eTools, and must be acknowledged in reports.

To establish the necessity and scope for a new resource, an *eTools review*, involving the classification and objective evaluation of the search results, follows the contextual review. The Mobile App Rating Scale (MARS) is a reliable tool for undertaking this step. It facilitates expert rating of the eTool's visual design, functionality, and consistency with evidence-based interventions. Existing high-quality eTools should be reviewed to identify functionality and design concepts for the new eTool. These examples cue discussions across the team on scope, budget and timeframes of the project.

In the next phase, *participatory design workshops* engage prospective users directly in the creative decision-making process, to maximise the uptake, usage and impact of the new tool. A user group examines and provides feedback on shortlisted eTools, and offers suggestions for improvement, in the context of their own experience of managing the focal health issue. This generates design concepts which are iteratively refined through consultation to become preliminary design requirements.

*Expert concept design* then juxtaposes ideas from the participatory design workshops with those of an expert team with requisite intervention, design and IT knowledge to produce wireframes. These are used to refine eTool design and prioritise potential functions in line with preliminary requirements. All experts are engaged in this process, to ensure communication of interdisciplinary perspectives.

The next phase is iterative design and development. Ideas from the expert team are discussed in further participatory design workshops to refine the design and functionality of the eTool. A prototype is then presented to prospective users for qualitative and quantitative evaluations, the latter facilitated by measures such as the app user version of the MARS. The eTool is also evaluated on a screen-by-screen basis to highlight targets for final editing resulting in a beta version.

The final two phases are user testing and outcome evaluation. These phases can be accomplished in parallel, as use of the eTool will both allow beta testing (based on users' ratings of eTool acceptability, perceived utility, relevance and value) and observations of outcomes. Ideally, this outcome evaluation should include one or more RCTs, as the gold standard for efficacy assessment. Between-groups trials including a short-term delayed access group or comparison with an alternate eTool can often be undertaken quickly and at relatively low cost. In the absence of a RCT, minimum data should include usage metrics and pre-post changes for a substantial sample of users on a psychometrically sound measure. Independent expert raters may also be asked to evaluate the tool on a standard measure such as the MARS.

The authors have now undertaken the development of several eTools using the above procedure, including RCTs. The Ray's Night Out app increased young people's alcohol-related knowledge and decreased typical and maximum alcohol consumption. The Music eScape app helped users identify connections between mood and music, and improve their mood. The Keep it Real interactive website reduced the frequency of both psychotic-like experiences and cannabis use. Trials are nearing completion on a web intervention promoting the wellbeing of first-time parents (Baby Steps), and the Breakup Shakeup app targeting relationship breakup distress in adolescents. When the procedure was applied to mindfulness eTools, an existing high-quality app, Smiling Mind, was identified in contextual review using the MARS. In an RCT, the app gave differential improvements in the mental wellbeing and distress of young people.

## Clinical Implications

Use of this seven-stage eTool development and evaluation process affords practitioners and users more confidence in an eTool's real world effectiveness in supporting mental health and wellbeing. By consulting prospective users throughout the process, developers produce an eTool that is aesthetically pleasing, easy to use and relevant to the target population, increasing the likelihood of its uptake.

## Future Directions

Streamlining the development of CBT eTools, while retaining an emphasis on evidentiary support, enables an adaptable and responsive approach to eHealth opportunities. If widespread agreement can be reached on a procedure such as ours, and if fulfilment of its features can be disseminated widely, confidence in eTools by practitioners, funders and the community would be greatly enhanced.

## Further Readings

Bakker, D., Kazantzis, N., Rickwood, D., & Rickard, N. (2016). Mental Health Smartphone Apps: Review and Evidence-Based Recommendations for Future Developments. *JMIR Mental Health, 3*(1), e7.

Mani, M., Kavanagh, D. J., Hides, L., & Stoyanov, S. R. (2015). Review and Evaluation of Mindfulness-Based iPhone Apps. *JMIR mHealth and uHealth, 3*(3).

Stoyanov, S. R., Hides, L., Kavanagh, D. J., Zelenko, O., Tjondronegoro, D., & Mani, M. (2015). Mobile app rating scale: a new tool for assessing the quality of health mobile apps. *JMIR mHealth and uHealth, 3*(1).

Chapter 46

# From research to implementation: The eCentreClinic and MindSpot Clinic

Nickolai Titov, Lauren G. Staples, Vincent J. Fogliati, and Blake F. Dear

## Overview

Anxiety and depressive disorders are highly prevalent and disabling. Unfortunately, many people have difficulty accessing conventional mental health services for a range of reasons, including stigma, the limited availability of mental health professionals, and the costs of treatment. Some of these barriers may be overcome by delivering psychological treatments via the internet. Evidence from controlled research trials has demonstrated that when guided by a therapist, internet-based cognitive-behaviour therapy (iCBT) for adults with symptoms of anxiety and depression is clinically efficacious, cost-effective, and acceptable to participants. However, evidence for the effectiveness of iCBT treatments when administered as part of routine care is currently limited.

This chapter describes a systematic body conducted at two online facilities based at Macquarie University, Sydney, Australia: the eCentreClinic (www.ecentreclinic.org.au), a specialist research unit that develops and evaluates iCBT interventions for adults with symptoms of anxiety and depression; and the MindSpot Clinic (www.mindspot.org.au), a national mental health service funded by the Australian Government to deliver the interventions to adults across Australia.

## Major Findings

The six randomised controlled trials (RCTs) described here followed an earlier series of RCTs conducted at the eCentreClinic which had the aim of developing three different iCBT interventions: (1) the Mood Mechanic Course for adults aged 18 to 25 years; (2) the Wellbeing Course for adults aged 18 to 60; and (3) the Wellbeing Plus Course for adults aged 60 and older. These courses were developed via an iterative process of evaluation and improvement aimed at optimising their acceptability and efficacy. Each course was developed as a transdiagnostic intervention that aimed to reduce common symptoms of anxiety and depressive disorders in different age groups.

More than 1500 participants were recruited for the final six RCTs, which used minimal exclusion criteria in an attempt to represent the actual populations who would eventually use the courses. The designs of each RCT were informed by the evidence available for each iCBT intervention. For the Mood Mechanic Course ($n = 180$), a two-group treatment vs waitlist control design was used, reflecting the relatively early phase of development. The RCT of the Wellbeing Plus Course ($n = 433$), earlier versions of which had been previously evaluated in four clinical trials, involved a three-parallel-group design comparing access to the course with weekly therapist support, or self-guided access to the course either with or without an initial interview with a therapist. The four RCTs of the Wellbeing Course ($n = 965$) represented a more complex design comprising people with either a principal diagnosis of major depressive disorder, generalised anxiety disorder, social anxiety disorder, or panic disorder. Participants were randomly allocated to receive either a disorder-specific or transdiagnostic iCBT intervention, either with or without therapist support. Taken together, these RCTs compared two dominant models of therapy and two dominant models of support, over a 2-year period, the results of which would be important to their eventual roll-out in routine clinical settings.

Notwithstanding the differences in population and design, the results of each RCT described here were consistent. Significant clinical improvements were observed across all treatment conditions and all age groups. These improvements were observed across multiple validated clinical measures for each disorder, as measured by effect sizes (Cohen's $d > 1.0$), percentage change in symptoms, or reliable clinical change estimates, with gains sustained up to two years after treatment. Importantly, deterioration rates were consistently low, and satisfaction rates were high across the trials.

The three iCBT interventions: Mood Mechanic, Wellbeing, and Wellbeing Plus, were subsequently implemented at the MindSpot Clinic, a national online mental health service. To date, these interventions have been administered to more than 10,000 adults aged 18 to 95 years, from across Australia. Importantly, the outcomes obtained at MindSpot have closely replicated the results from the clinical trials, and have produced consistently large effect sizes and high levels of patient satisfaction. These results provide an exciting example of how interventions developed in research environments can be successfully implemented into everyday care.

## Clinical Implications

The described body of work has important clinical implications. First, it demonstrates that psychological interventions can be successfully translated from controlled research environments to routine clinical settings. Second, it demonstrates the effectiveness of both transdiagnostic and disorder-specific psychological interventions for symptoms of anxiety and depression. Third, it shows that carefully developed psychological interventions can be successfully delivered with low levels of therapist support. In combination, this work raises important questions about the nature of psychotherapeutic process and the mechanisms of treatment, especially where significant clinical improvements are observed with little or no clinical contact. Such outcomes remind us of the importance of reflecting on the function of therapy and the therapist, and the potential impact of well written and presented therapeutic materials.

## Future Directions

Outstanding questions include whether the transdiagnostic paradigm can be broadened to other psychological disorders or to psychological distress related to chronic health conditions. These questions have important clinical and theoretical implications. Effective transdiagnostic interventions will simplify treatment planning and delivery. Further, treatments that effectively treat a broad range of conditions will inform improvements in diagnostic and classificatory systems.

Additional questions concern how to optimally combine iCBT and similar approaches into everyday clinical practice and existing systems of mental health care. We are aware of research that is exploring this question, and, in collaborative projects with several external clinical units we have demonstrated that such integration is possible. However, we note that this work is still at a relatively early stage and that the requirements of individual health services need to be considered.

## Further Reading

Andersson, G., & Titov, N. (2014). Advantages and limitations of internet-based interventions for common mental disorders. *World Psychiatry, 13,* 4–11.

Kazdin, A.E., & Blase, S.L. (2011). Rebooting Psychotherapy Research and Practice to Reduce the Burden of Mental Illness. *Perspectives on Psychological Science 6,* 21–37.

Titov, N., Dear, B.F., Staples, L.G., Bennett-Levy, J., Klein., B., Rapee, R.M., ... Nielssen, O.B. (2015). MindSpot Clinic: An accessible, efficient, and effective online treatment service for anxiety and depression. *Psychiatric Services, 66,* 1043–1050.

Chapter 47

# Healthy mind, healthy body: Recent advances in internet-delivered interventions for chronic physical conditions and their comorbidities

Jill M. Newby

## Overview

Chronic physical conditions such as chronic pain, osteoarthritis and diabetes, and cancer are some of the leading causes of disability in Australia. People with chronic physical conditions are at increased risk for developing mental health problems, and often have high rates of anxiety and depression. Having comorbid physical and mental health problems reduces quality of life, affects an individual's ability to self-manage their condition, and can even predict poor long-term prognosis. Cognitive-behaviour therapy (CBT) is considered to be the gold standard evidence-based treatment for chronic pain, and anxiety and depression in the context of chronic physical conditions. However, treatment barriers (e.g., cost, stigma), long waiting lists, and the lack of trained clinicians (especially in rural areas of Australia) prevent many individuals from seeking and receiving effective treatment. Delivering CBT via the internet with clinician guidance provides a novel cost-effective way to address these barriers, and improve access to treatment for people who cannot attend or afford face-to-face treatment, or those with physical issues restricting their mobility. There have been recent advances in research into internet-delivered interventions and prevention programs for people with chronic physical conditions. The conditions that can be successfully treated and managed online include chronic pain, illness anxiety, irritable bowel syndrome (IBS), osteoarthritis and cancer-distress.

## Major Findings

Internet-delivered cognitive-behaviour therapy (iCBT) interventions and multidisciplinary treatment programs delivered online have been shown to be an effective, reliable and acceptable treatment option for individuals with a range of chronic health conditions. The most widely researched iCBT interventions are in the context of chronic pain and IBS, however, there are also many chronic disease self-management programs that teach individuals living with heart disease, lung disease, diabetes, and other diseases to better manage their lifestyle and symptoms to live a healthier life. There is now evidence that iCBT is effective for reducing pain-related distress and improving self-efficacy in chronic pain populations, reducing cancer-related distress, reducing anxiety about health, and in treating headaches and sexual dysfunction. iCBT also presents a viable treatment option for people suffering from depression in the context of physical conditions, including osteoarthritis and diabetes.

Despite these positive findings, the uptake of CBT, whether it is delivered face-to-face or via the internet is poor in outpatient medical clinics where the focus is on physical health not mental health. For example, up to half of individuals who meet criteria for depression in diabetes clinics do not seek treatment for their mental health problem, despite the potentially positive role that iCBT may play in reducing their depression and improving their confidence in managing their physical condition. In addition, due to pragmatic and systems-related barriers internet CBT for the self-management of chronic diseases are rarely incorporated as part of routine care within outpatient clinics.

## Clinical Implications

Identification of distress, depression and anxiety in the context of physical illness is not enough to promote change. Proactive treatment is needed to minimise the risk of long-term impairment, disability and distress. iCBT is an affordable, accessible treatment option for individuals living with chronic physical problems, and can be used to provide critical education and tools for self-management, as well as reduce depression and anxiety that may be experienced as a comorbid and complicating presenting issue. iCBT also is an excellent tool to use within routine clinical practice, as it provides a tool to assist in monitoring and tracking the progress of patients between face-to-face appointments so that any deterioration in symptoms or wellbeing can be managed proactively. Clinically, iCBT is a tool in many different ways including as a stand-alone intervention, as a complement to existing treatment such as being offered in conjunction with face-to-face treatment, or as relapse prevention tool to maintain gains after intensive multidisciplinary interventions.

## Future Directions

Future research should focus on exploring how to improve the uptake of internet interventions in medical settings from primary care to outpatient medical clinics, by identifying and addressing barriers to implementation at the individual, practitioner, and health service level. Future research will benefit from evaluating the impact of internet treatments within a stepped-care model of treatment delivery, evaluation of interventions designed to treat multiple comorbidities as well as interventions specific tailored to physical health problems. By offering iCBT as an early intervention tool to educate patients about their disease and how to self-manage and maintain their resilience, this has potential to prevent the development of disability and reduced workforce participation arising from physical health issues. Future research will benefit from identifying the optimal methods to keep clients engaged in internet therapy to maximise their outcomes and maintain physical and mental health. Finally, future research will benefit from understanding the mechanisms of therapeutic change and improvements during internet CBT, including at a biological, physiological and psychological level to understand how iCBT improves both the body and the mind.

## Further Readings

Hedman, E., Ljotsson, B., & Lindefors, N. (2012). Cognitive behavior therapy via the Internet: A systematic review of applications, clinical efficacy and cost-effectiveness. *Expert Review of Pharmacoeconomics & Outcomes Research, 12*(6), 745–764. doi: 10.1586/erp.12.67

Van Bastelaar, K., Cuijpers, P., Pouwer, F., Riper, H., & Snoek, F. J. (2011). Development and reach of a web-based cognitive behavioural therapy programme to reduce symptoms of depression and diabetes-specific distress. *Patient Education and Counseling; Patient Education and Counseling, 84*(1), 49–55. doi: 10.1016/j.pec.2010.06.013

Section 13

Training, Practice and Access Issues

Chapter 48

# Advancing the evidence for therapeutic process as a necessary condition for cognitive-behaviour therapy outcomes

Nikolaos Kazantzis, Keith S. Dobson, and Stefan G. Hofmann

## Overview

The therapeutic relationship has been considered a necessary, but not a sufficient condition for the effective practice of cognitive-behaviour therapy (CBT). Every clinician knows that empathy, trust, a strong alliance, and unconditional positive regard are necessary to engage clients in therapy. What may be less understood are the CBT specific aspects of the client–therapist relationship, which are embedded in the techniques and strategies of CBT. In this chapter, we offer a clinician-oriented account of the evidence regarding the therapeutic relationship in CBT, with a particular focus on engagement issues.

Our collaborative work at the Cognitive Behaviour Therapy Research Unit (http://www.med.monash.edu.au/ psych/cbtru/) housed within the Monash Institute of Cognitive and Clinical Neurosciences and School of Psychological Sciences at Monash University in Australia, aims to understand what makes CBT an effective treatment for mental health problems, to enhance CBT using available evidence, and to translate those results to the practitioner community.

## Major Findings

The human interaction of psychotherapy is an exceedingly complex phenomenon. As intimated above, there are generic (or 'common') elements of the therapeutic interaction that may be found in a range of therapy modalities. A therapy bond, comprised of mutual respect, trust, warmth, and positive regard are foundational for this interaction. Two other fundamental elements of the therapeutic relationship include client-therapist agreement on the goals of therapy, and the selection of tasks needed in order to attain those goals. These latter two elements are not specific to CBT, but they are still important for CBT. In fact, another construct, the 'alliance' is generally operationalised as comprising bond, as well as the agreement on goals and therapy tasks.

Elements of the relationship that are specific to CBT include collaboration — active shared work between the client and therapist in the design, conduct, and evaluation of techniques. When CBT was conceived, collaboration was considered a distinguishing feature between CBT and psychoanalysis, and other modalities of the time. However, the collaboration was important insofar as it represented shared work in the empirical exploration of the clients' beliefs system — either their process or content in thinking. A further element of collaboration is Socratic dialogue, which is the use of guided questions to help the client to discover new ideas and conclusions. These CBT specific elements reveal that the concepts of 'relationship' and 'technique' are not neatly distinguished, as collaborative empiricism and Socratic dialogue are both interventions and relationship elements.

Most of the literature on CBT process had focused on client engagement with between-session interventions, also referred to as 'homework.' Unfortunately the term 'homework' often has negative connotations, and may convey the idea that such interventions are directives, which could therefore be associated with the potential for 'failure' in the therapeutic process.

The evidence, however, is clear that homework enhances CBT outcomes. Homework promotes client engagement (also sometimes referred to as 'adherence'), which is itself associated with symptom reduction. Our research team has conducted several meta-analytic reviews of this evidence, and our most recent review raises the question about whether skill acquisition should be regularly assessed alongside adherence.

Our group has also conducted surveys among practitioners, and in Australia, Germany, New Zealand, and the United States two things have become clear. First, practitioners frequently use homework. Unfortunately, they do not necessarily support clients to develop a specific homework plan in the manner recommended in our clinical practice guides.

We have also constructed a protocol to engage clients in homework, and tested it in community, clinic, and randomised control trial contexts. These data are also clear. When therapists skillfully integrate this protocol (defined as collaborative, connected to case conceptualisation, and flexibly adapted, but specific) client beliefs about the homework are more favorable, more homework is completed, and symptoms are reduced.

We have expanded this interest on engagement to include in-session engagement, and have shown that when techniques are more tailored for clients (i.e., there is higher levels of collaborative empiricism and Socratic dialogue), CBT shows sustained benefit. What is particularly important about these data is that we controlled for the working alliance when evaluating these relations with outcome.

## Clinical Implications

Our theoretical and empirical work yields a profound conclusion regarding the therapeutic relationship in CBT, which is that the relationship is just as important in CBT as it is for other models of psychotherapy. Our work suggests a focus on the skill of the clinician in collaboration and individualising techniques for clients, in order to maximise motivation and engagement with interventions between sessions. Finally, our work suggests that clinical training and supervision in CBT need to emphasise CBT specific elements of the therapeutic interaction (e.g., collaborative empiricism and Socratic dialogue), and how these elements warrant special attention in the development of skill and competence in advanced CBT practice.

## Future Directions

Most of the research on the process of CBT has focused on static assessments of therapy process as predictors of subsequent symptom change. This research method is limited, as therapy processes fluctuate during sessions, and dynamically relate to symptom change over the course of therapy. Further, client characteristics moderate the relations between process and outcome, and therapist skill and other important processes need to be considered within our analytic models. An important research direction is to utilise more sophisticated methodologies, which can account for the array of variables that intersect in the prediction of outcome in CBT.

**Further Readings**

Kazantzis, N., Dattilio, F. M., & Dobson, K. S. (2016). *The therapeutic relationship in cognitive behavior therapy: The heart and soul of effective practice.* New York, NY: Guilford.

Kazantzis, N., Deane, F. P., Ronan, K. R., & L'Abate, L. (Eds.). (2005). *Using homework assignments in cognitive behavioral therapy.* New York, NY: Routledge.

Chapter 49

# Improving access to psychological therapies (IAPT) in Australia: Evidence-based cognitive-behaviour therapy interventions for anxiety, depression and gambling addiction

Paul Cromarty

## Overview

In the United Kingdom (UK), the pioneering Improving Access to Psychological Therapies (IAPT) program is an attempt to enact National Institute for Health and Clinical Excellence (NICE) guidelines for commonly occurring mental health problems. Australian initiatives mirror this with structured training and adherence to proven interventions. The interaction between clinical practice, theory, outcome research and experimental evidence, in Australian models, aims toward a coordinated effort to develop and maintain truly empirically grounded services. Typically, IAPT services such as *beyondblue's* NewAccess program, target mild to moderate depression and specific anxiety disorders benefitting from Low Intensity Cognitive-Behaviour Therapy (LiCBT). Australian IAPT has been adapted to novel settings, including emergency departments, discharge from hospital and cardiac rehab. It can be applied to chronic health conditions and specific disorders like problem gambling, effectively a commonly occurring mental health problem in Australia, that evidence shows responds to both behavioural and cognitive paradigms. All initiatives are piloted within a 'stepped care model' in small innovative services with a core team of CBT trainers and supervisors. Thus allowing tightly scaffold clinical systems with a high degree of treatment fidelity and monitoring of outcomes. Steps are required beyond the pilots to nationally roll out evidence-based services, informed by theoretical advances, and framework of ongoing research and evaluation.

## Major Findings

IAPT focuses on maintaining treatment fidelity in services, allowing clients to access evidence-based interventions with optimal recovery rates. Clinical outcomes are designed to match those normally observed in randomised controlled trials, that research shows do not always translate as effectively into standard CBT services. This is despite no significant differences in client symptoms and that therapists in services tend to be more experienced clinicians than those delivering research protocols.

Adaptations, including training of non-health professionals, use of disruptive technologies to self-refer and deliver supervision, have not diluted the effectiveness of the model. High recovery rates in Australian IAPT are evaluated by the demanding metric of being below caseness on measures of anxiety and depression, after 6 sessions of LiCBT. This transparency must be viewed in the context of traditional mental health services in western cultures failing to uniformly provide evidence-based treatments or measures of clinical effectiveness. In stark contrast to IAPT, mental health services historically focus on waiting times and throughput alone rather than actual recovery. They are not uniformly subjected to rigorous key performance indicators (KPIs) such as functional recovery, loss of diagnosis and return to employment. Given this, on top of time and costs of training health professionals, longer term human and economic benefits of IAPT may prove even greater.

A functioning IAPT service is 'self-correcting' which is essential in stepped care, with referrals that are unsuitable or unresponsive, stepped-up to more appropriate interventions such as High Intensity Cognitive-Behaviour Therapy (HiCBT) delivered by trained health professionals. Frequently monitored KPIs are impaired if adherence to suitability criteria and proven treatments is not maintained. The systematic approach to treatment fidelity and 'service model fidelity' should be applied to IAPT as integral to enhancing quality of interventions, client's safety, and experiences within the system. These functions are required to tightly scaffold clinical systems and match improvements achieved in research.

Detailed data is generated by these services, with all outcome measures applied each session. This allows mapping of change processes with greater frequency and in more detail than many randomised controlled trials of CBT. This, in turn, is used to continually inform theory and practice by analysis of data, wherein relationships between treatment and outcomes vary by service, supervisors and coaches.

### Clinical Implications

Against the intuition of many experienced psychologists (myself included), evidence shows that effective interventions can be delivered by non-health professionals with a short, intensive training period. It requires structure, clear protocols and regular clinical supervision, all delivered within a stepped-care framework. This facilitates development of 'focused expertise' without requiring a breadth of experience in mental health settings or professions. The same competency based, regularly supervised LiCBT training for coaches and HiCBT training for health professionals is widespread in the UK. Psychologists, psychiatrists and mental health nurses are required to complete post-basic training in CBT before accreditation as specialists. To date, there is only one multidisciplinary Masters Level CBT course in Australia.

The phenomenon of therapeutic drift increases as clinicians gain more experience and confidence. This drift from the evidence base impairs clinical recovery rates, leading to services not replicating results from research. Attempting to be eclectic in delivering interventions actually impairs recovery rates. In contrast 'high dose and narrow bandwidth' interventions, repeatedly targeting the primary problem, enhances recovery rates and sees gains generalise to comorbid states. There is an ethical obligation for experienced clinicians to provide interventions based on evidence over individual opinion. Frequent clinical supervision has a role in maintaining this, and treatment fidelity among supervisors is equally important. Ongoing clinical supervision, delivered using a computerised case management system with internet and telephone based contact has proven successful in Australia where there are often vast distances between supervisors, services and clients. Proven clinical interventions already exist but if these fail to translate into front line services, it is the system that is far more likely to be responsible than the evidence base.

### Future Directions

For IAPT to roll out optimally across Australian Primary Health Networks, as a first-step service, key actions are required. These are a national oversight committee, curriculum, competency framework, training provider, supervisor criteria, service model and KPIs. The same IAPT competency-based training and services should be extended to introduce an equivalent level of rigour for high intensity (HiCBT) services, as the next step in the mental health system. In stepped care CBT services, training for coaches and health professionals should be linked, with HiCBT training more widely available at postgraduate level for psychologists and other health professionals. A pathway should be developed for accreditation and recognition of LiCBT coaches as a new health profession. Advances requiring wholesale change, can pose an initial threat to traditional services and professions. Innovations can ultimately fail to have an impact in wider health settings if they are not resourced, implemented and managed successfully.

## Further Readings

Cromarty, P., Drummond, A., Francis, T., Watson J., & Battersby, M. (2016). NewAccess for depression and anxiety: Adapting the UK Improving Access to Psychological Therapies program across Australia. *Australasian Psychiatry*. doi: 10.1177/1039856216641310

Koivu, B., Drummond, A., Battersby, M., & Cromarty, P. (2016). Large reductions in depression and anxiety via low intensity CBT delivered by novice coach. *Australian & New Zealand Journal of Psychiatry*. doi:10.1177/0004867415624971

Shafran, R., Clark, D.M., Fairburn, C.G., Arntz, A., Barlow, D.H., Ehlers, A., … Wilson, G.T. (2009) Mind the gap: Improving the dissemination of CBT. *Behaviour Research and Therapy, 47,* 902–909.

Chapter 50

# Implementation of evidence-based interventions: Barriers and opportunities

Erica Crome, Andrew Baillie, Maree Teesson, Frances Kay-Lambkin and Mark Deady

## Overview

Significant advances have been made in the development and evaluation of empirically supported interventions for mental disorders. However, there remains a gap between research and practice settings, with only a minority of people seeking treatment for mental disorders receiving gold-standard care. Interventions with strong support in research trials may take decades to become commonplace in clinical settings, if at all. This has prompted an increased emphasis on research to understand the factors that facilitate and interfere with the dissemination and implementation of empirically supported treatments, as well as innovations to reduce implementation barriers.

## Major Findings

One of the most influential factors determining whether or not an empirically supported intervention is adopted or sustained in health care settings is cost. This is consistent with theories of the diffusion of innovations, particularly the need for potential end-users to have sufficient resources to adopt and sustain use of a novel technology or procedure. There are diffuse costs associated with implementing empirically supported treatments for mental disorders, with these costs borne by a range of stakeholders. These include costs of production (e.g., pharmaceutical manufacturing), practitioners' services and incidental costs associated with accessing treatment (e.g., travel, time off work). There are also likely to be significant training costs associated with disseminating complex procedural interventions, such as psychological therapies.

Psychological therapies, particularly cognitive-behavioural therapies, are often the most effective and cost-effective treatments for common mental disorders. Ensuring that results reported in research trials are achieved in clinical settings requires a detailed understanding of the theoretical basis of therapies, techniques for delivery and adaptations for complex presentations such as comorbid disorders. This requires a combination of didactic (e.g., reading manuals, attending workshops) and experiential (e.g., role play, supervision) training. Training is likely to result in direct costs (e.g., trainer fees), as well as indirect costs associated with time away from usual duties. These indirect costs may be experienced as lost income for private practitioners, or the cost of locum staff or reduced service capabilities within larger organisations. Costing these direct and indirect costs within a hypothetical model highlights that, using current market rates for training materials and income, training costs can be almost equivalent to an annual income for some health professionals. Clearly, these costs are unfeasible and unsustainable.

The Internet has vast potential for reducing the costs associated with disseminating and implementing novel psychological interventions. The ability to deliver standardised content means that interventions can be easily scaled-up to reach large numbers of people, with little impact on quality. Online therapies supported by brief therapist contact (e.g., phone, email) are often more effective than purely self-directed treatments; however, these contacts still require substantially less time and training than face-to-face treatment. Reduced therapist inputs translate to reduced costs for consumers and/or funding agencies. There is growing evidence that online platforms may also fill a significant gap in early intervention, drug education and screening programs on a population level. They even hold the promise of more cost-effective training, with interactive training programs, webinar series and online communities increasing access to training at reduced costs.

However, as online platforms are still relatively novel, there is still much to learn about optimising outcomes from these interventions and understanding their role in the mental health system. Surprisingly, the uptake of online interventions in the general community has been lower than anticipated, with some consumers reporting concerns about the privacy of their data or feeling online treatments were impersonal. It is also unclear how important treatment factors, such as therapeutic alliance, differ between face-to-face and online formats. Moreover, it is unclear how online therapies should be integrated in usual care. Novel frameworks to improve uptake of online interventions appear to improve engagement, with examples including referral to online interventions coordinated through general practitioners. However, it is unclear whether these referrals should act as an adjunct to specialised care, or act as a gateway to specialised services in stepped-care models. In order to realise the potential of these technologies, research is required to understand how they can be used most effectively within the broad health environment.

## Clinical Implications

Improving the implementation of empirically supported treatments is essential for realising the potential benefits offered by advances in treatments for mental disorders. After all, even the best treatment will only ever be as effective as our ability to implement it. This is likely to require a coordinated effort across multiple sectors; including consumers, health practitioners, researchers and policy makers. Innovations that reduce the costs of dissemination and implementation are likely to be power levers for closing the gap between research and practice. Online therapies are one method for reducing the costs of implementing empirically supported treatments; however, an understanding of how these technologies can be used most effectively is still emerging.

## Future Directions

Research to clarify how online therapies can become more integrated into existing health systems may maximise return on investments in these technologies. This includes understanding how to address barriers to accessing online therapies (e.g., privacy concerns, motivation), as well as understanding where these technologies should be placed in pathways of care. Finally, as most of the investment in online technologies has been directed at supporting consumers, further research into using technology to deliver training to the existing workforce is likely to be fruitful.

## Further Readings

Crome, E., Shaw, J., & Baillie, A. (2016). Costs and returns on training investment for empirically supported psychological interventions. *Australian Health Review.* doi: 10.1071/AH15129

Newton, N. C., Teesson, M., Vogl, L. E., & Andrews, G. (2010). Internet based prevention for alcohol and cannabis use: final results of the Climate Schools course. *Addiction, 105*(4), 749–759.

Meurk, C., Leung, J., Hall, W., Head, B. W., & Whiteford, H. (2016). Establishing and governing e-mental health care in Australia: A systematic review of challenges and a call for policy-focused research. *Journal of Medical Internet Research, 18*(1), e10.

Chapter 51

# Understanding, assessing and treating mental health disorders in older adults

Viviana M. Wuthrich and Sunil Bhar

## Overview

Soon there will be a greater number of older adults over the age of 65 years than ever before. The ageing of the world's population will call for an increased understanding of, and treatments for, mental health disorders in older populations. The health workforce of the future will require upskilling to address the needs of older adults. Cognitive decline and dementia incidence increases with age, and depression and anxiety are common problems in older adults, yet they remain poorly detected and treated conditions. This chapter reports on advances in understanding mental health conditions in older adults, in assessment and treatment methods tailored for these populations, and in training programs in geropsychology for the health care sector of the future.

## Major Findings

Depression and anxiety are the most prominent mental health disorders in older adult populations with up to 24% of community dwelling older adults experiencing clinical levels of depression and 10% experiencing clinical levels of anxiety. Rates of depression and anxiety in older adults living in residential aged care facilities (RACFs) are even higher with estimates of 50% for depression and 3% to 20% for anxiety disorders. Untreated depression and anxiety in older adults is associated with severe consequences including increased mortality, morbidity, disability, medication and service use, risk for cognitive decline and dementia, and decreased wellbeing. In RACFs untreated depression and anxiety is further associated with increased reports of pain, functional deficits, sub-nutrition, staff stress, direct nursing time, care needs and behavioural disturbances. Cognitive decline and dementia are also mental disorders that become increasingly common with incidence increasing as age increases, from initial prevalence of 1% of under 65 year olds to 28% of 100 year olds, and are also frequently comorbid with depression and anxiety. More evidence-based treatment for depression and anxiety in older adults with and without cognitive decline are needed. Further given there are no successful treatments for dementia, interventions to prevent or slow cognitive decline in at-risk individuals are desperately needed.

There is evidence that depression and anxiety present somewhat differently as people age, and emotional symptoms are commonly misattributed to physical problems in this age group. This makes the identification and assessment of these disorders more difficult by both untrained professionals and individuals themselves. Further, age and cohort specific characteristics such as normal cognitive declines in memory and processing speed, mean that assessment tools and psychotherapeutic approaches may need to be adapted for this age group. Some progress has been made in developing age appropriate assessment tools that can be used to measure emotional symptoms in older populations in a range of older adult settings, including RACFs (e.g., the Geriatric Anxiety Inventory, Geriatric Depression Scale, Cornell Scale for Depression in Dementia); however, more work is needed including identifying robust clinical cut-offs and defining guidelines for diagnostic remission on these measures.

Treating depression and anxiety in older adults may be particularly important as there is recent evidence that depression and anxiety are associated with increased risk for the development of cognitive decline and dementia. Recent estimates suggest that accounting for shared variance among all potentially modifiable risks for dementia (such as low education/mental stimulation, low social stimulation, physical inactivity, smoking, excessive alcohol use, poor diet), the population attributable risk related to depression specifically is 11%, with emerging evidence for anxiety contributing further to the risk. Given expected increases in the prevalence of cognitive decline and dementia as the population ages, there have been recent calls to develop prevention programs to reduce this risk. Cognitive-behaviourial therapy programs have already been demonstrated to be efficacious for treating depression and anxiety in older adults in community and medical settings. Promisingly, there is emerging evidence that cognitive-behaviour therapy (CBT) coupled with motivational interviewing can be used to treat both depression and anxiety as well as other health and lifestyle risks for dementia. This program, developed by Dr Viviana Wuthrich, has been shown to lead to reductions in a number of risk factors, and has the potential to reduce the expected rates of conversion to dementia in at-risk older adults.

Finally, it has been repeatedly shown that many psychologists feel ill-equipped to assess and treat older adult clients; however, studies have shown that exposing students to older adult populations increases their confidence and desire to work with them. In order to prepare for the increased needs that will be placed on mental health services, changes to the models of training are needed. A novel training program for provisional psychologists implemented in RACFs resulted in significant improvements in student confidence and geropsychology knowledge, while also being well received by residents. This study demonstrates the feasibility of training programs situated in RACFs, and their positive impact on trainee health care professionals to better prepare them for working with older adults.

## Clinical Implications

The results presented in this chapter increase our understanding of differences in emotional distress in older and younger adults in a medical setting, report on the development of clinical guidelines for assessing clinical recovery from anxiety and depressive disorders, report on preliminary results of a novel CBT program to reduce risk for cognitive decline and dementia in at-risk older adults, and provide evidence for a training model to increase student's knowledge of clinical geropsychology and confidence in treating older adults living in RACFs.

## Future Directions

In summary, the numbers of adults over the age of 65 years will soon surge, and with increased longevity, more people will live beyond the age of 65. There are particularly strong needs to develop and translate into real-world settings evidence-based treatment programs to target mental health in older adults, evaluate programs to reduce risk for cognitive decline and dementia, and to build better training models to train mental health professionals to work with older adults across a range of settings.

## Further Readings

Bhar, S.S., Silver, M., Campbell, J., Lawson, M., O'Brien, S., & Rehm, I. (2015). Counselling older adults living in residential aged care settings: Four illustrative case studies. *Australian Psychologist, 50*(2), 141–147. doi: 10.1111/ap.12098

Pachana, N.A., & Laidlaw, K. (Eds.) (2014). *The Oxford handbook of clinical geropsychology.* Oxford, England: Oxford University Press.

Wuthrich, V.M., Rapee, R.M., Kangas, M., & Perini, S. (2016). Randomised controlled trial of group cognitive behavioural therapy compared to a discussion group for comorbid anxiety and depression in older adults. *Psychological Medicine, 46*(4), 785–795. doi:10.1017/S0033291715002251

Chapter 52

# Evaluating cognitive-behaviour therapy in private practice settings

Monica O'Kelly, Kathryn Gilson and James Collard

## Overview

This chapter discusses the importance of practice-based research for the development of the psychological profession. It focuses on three models of research that practitioners in private practice can contribute to and engage in. The benefits of these models to bridging the current knowledge gap from randomised control trials to typical private practice settings and their role in helping to further inform future psychological practice is highlighted. The advantages for the individual practitioner are also emphasised. Finally, the chapter closes by discussing how the development of this type of research can be encouraged.

## Major Findings

There is considerable research involving randomised controlled trials (RCT) demonstrating the efficacy of cognitive-behaviour therapy (CBT). Given the considerable difference between everyday clinical practice and research settings in which the studies are usually carried out it cannot be assumed that such therapeutic approaches will translate effectively to the private practice setting. While it can be challenging to conduct research in private practice settings, it is an important aspect of evidence-based practice. Engaging in such research can help to enhance clinical practice, and strengthen the validity of RCT findings, while also helping clinicians to stay current with research advances.

Traditionally evidence-based practice has as its basis the results of RCTs conducted in university settings. In these RCTs individuals are generally screened for one psychological problem, with strict exclusion criteria, limiting comorbidities and other confounding factors. In addition specific protocols for a targeted mental illness are followed (often verbatim) from manuals, therapy is delivered by specifically trained therapists, which may be very experienced professors or young graduate students, and the clients do not pay for treatment or may even be given financial incentives to take part. These conditions do not apply in private practice settings where comorbidities are the norm and clients are paying for the service.

At present, there is a dearth of research to bridge this gap. This is an unfortunate situation. Many clinicians that practice CBT have a background as scientist practitioners. There is however a tendency for clinicians to only use evidence-based literature to inform treatment, rather than acquiring practice-based evidence, and contributing to the further development of the knowledge base.

Research in private practice can follow a number of different models. These include the evaluation of collated client data, case studies, and collaborations with research institutes, such as universities.

In studies involving the evaluation of collated client data it is important that clinicians consider their research questions, assessment tools, measurement times, consent forms, and ethical issues. Furthermore, in a multi-clinician study it is important that a uniform methodology for assessing presenting difficulties and client background, and treating client difficulties is established and followed. In developing a sample of client data in private practice it is likely that individuals will not present with the same psychological difficulties, however more general forms of assessing symptoms and distress can be used to develop a transdiagnostic sample to gather pooled data. For example, the Beck Depression Inventory (BDI-II) and the Depression Anxiety Stress Scales (DASS) can be used as general measures of symptom distress.

If conducting an intervention study through this type of research, it is not likely to be practical to provide the same manualised form of therapy for all clients, as client presentations are quite varied. It is important however that a single theoretical model, such as CBT, underpins that therapy provided. For an analysis of treatment effectiveness a base line and follow up time points need to be established (e.g., during, post, 1 month follow-up). This allows for the collation and statistical analysis of data from multiple clients.

With unique and complex presentations, it may be desirable to report on the intricacies of a specific presentation and how the client responds to treatment. This can be better researched in $N = 1$ case studies. These types of studies can utilise both qualitative and quantitative methods for reporting change. For qualitative methods, objective markers of behaviour change, subjective reports of cognitive and emotive changes, and medication reliance could all be reported. For more quantitative methods, change over time on psychometric instruments can be reported. It is also possible to demonstrate clinically significant change statistics using normative data from these standard measures.

Over recent years, in Australia, it has also become more common for universities to collaborate with private practitioners to conduct research. This has been a result of government funding of private psychological therapy, which has made it economically feasible to carry out such research. Specialised training is often provided for practitioners for the purpose of the study and ongoing support provided. Clients are recruited by the university in line with the study protocols and then referred to the practitioners. This allows for the recruitment of a larger number of individuals with a specific presenting difficulty and for the provision of treatment across a number of practitioners, helping to reduce any practitioner effects.

## Clinical Implications

These models of clinical research can help to bridge the gap from RCT efficacy studies to applied effectiveness studies. They allow for the gathering and the reporting of clinical findings from common private practice settings, from which psychological therapy is typically provided to the general public. The reporting of such research contributes to the development of the clinical knowledge base. In particular, it helps to address questions regarding the effectiveness of treatment with clients presenting with comorbid presentations, bridging the gap from RCTs based on a single psychopathology. The worth of such information should not be underestimated in helping to improve client outcomes for the future.

Engagement in practice research also has benefits for the practitioner. It can contribute to ongoing professional development, enabling and motivating the practitioner to keep up to date on current research and clinical findings and practices. Importantly, it also allows practitioners to obtain feedback on their therapeutic effectiveness, which can help to enhance their skills and credentials. In addition it can also enhance professional satisfaction and give the practitioner the opportunity to contribute to the development of the profession itself. In cases when collaborating with universities, the practitioner may receive expert training and supervision in a specific skill set.

## Future Directions

To promote the further development of practitioners as scientists and researchers who actively assess and report on their therapeutic effectiveness there is a need for practical supports. These include access to research databases, access to statistical analysis software, support with conducting statistical analyses, and support with developing publications. Furthermore, it is important that the value of this practice-based research be recognised by the scientific community, with accessible and suitable avenues for publication provided.

## Further Reading

Barlow, D.H., Nock, M.K., & Hersen, M. (2008). *Single case experimental designs: Strategies for studying behavior change* (3rd ed.). Boston, MA: Pearson Education.

Persons, J.B. (2007). Psychotherapists collect data during routine clinical work that can contribute to knowledge about mechanisms of change in psychotherapy. *Clinical Psychology: Science and Practice, 14*(3), 244–246.

Castonguay, L.G., Youn, S.J., Xiao, H., Muran, J.C., & Barber, J.P. (2015). Building clinicians–researchers partnerships: Lessons from diverse natural settings and practice-oriented initiatives. *Psychotherapy Research, 25*(1), 166–184.

Chapter 53

# Innovative cognitive-behaviour therapy: Is it the same in private practice and public health?

Gerri Minshall and Stephanie Allen

## Overview

The implementation of effective cognitive-behaviour therapy (CBT) is challenged and constrained by the setting in which it is being practiced. Implementation research investigates whether certain mental health problems (OCD, depression and so on) can be treated as effectively outside of a research setting. However, the focus of this chapter is more how the treatment (such as Dialectical Behaviour Therapy — DBT/CBT Enhanced for Eating Disorders) or specific CBT techniques (exposure being the clearest example) can be enacted in diverse settings. For the Australian context the most relevant settings to discuss are public health, whether mental or physical health, and private practice. Private practice implies a sole practitioner or a person primarily providing treatment alone — not as part of a team, although they may be practicing in a group private practice.

## Major Findings

The advantages of CBT are incredibly strong and useful and are already the focus of many books and conferences, including this one; CBT (1) has an extensive evidence base, (2) is applicable for a wide variety of mental health problems/physical health issues and life challenges, and (3) can be 'modified' to better suit different ages (adults/children/adolescents) and types of clients.

There are many CBT related constructs that cross different settings and presumably all seek to enhance the treatment provided — no matter the situation. These include (1) implementation research for particular disorders such as depression or eating disorders, (2) research on reflection/the supervisory relationship, (3) Nikolaos Kazantzis' work on the therapeutic relationship/encouraging homework in CBT, and (4) ideas around therapist competencies and training. Glenn Waller's publication on 'therapeutic drift' and how CBT can be changed from a 'doing therapy' into a 'talking therapy' due to the therapist's own weaknesses, is particularly useful.

But can CBT continue to be applied well in view of recent epic changes in the Australian system? According to the Australia's Health Workforce Series Psychologists in Focus, published by the Australian Government in 2012, about 41% of psychologists were employed in the public sector (this includes defence and education as well as health) and around 51% were employed in solo or group private practices. In 2006 Medicare started offering a rebate for psychological treatment and other psychological services. This has taken CBT out of public hospitals and put it in the realm of many sole practitioners. The contingencies are different in the different treatment settings and so it is possible that therapy is being shaped differently.

For example, public health frequently involves a multidisciplinary team that is specialised. Groups are certainly encouraged (more people being treated at once decreases waiting lists) and disorder specialisation is quite common. Parent Management Training or DBT Skills Training can be delivered in a group format, as originally conceptualised and researched. Medical backup for the physical components of an illness is frequently built in. (For instance, a physician or paediatrician assessing an eating disordered patient).

Sole practitioners on the other hand find it much more difficult to obtain treatment support from medical practitioners or enact any form of treatment not covered in the standard 50 to 60 minute individual session. But what about when core components of treatment are not included in a 50 to 60 minute session. For example, when working with children and adolescents it is quite common to have to make contact with the school and have multiple conversations/planning sessions for treatment and assessment? Should these be left out, charged for or done in the practitioner's own time? None of these proposed solutions are ideal. DBT prides itself on being effective with high risk patients and it requires a multi-component treatment — groups, individual therapy and telephone — coaching — essentially out of hours phone calls. It is also considered necessary to have a supportive team expert in the methodology.

## Clinical Implications

We know so little about comparing treatments in different clinical settings. It appears that DBT as researched and developed necessarily includes a skills training component and more than one clinician.

In public health, sometimes the number of sessions required for a CBT treatment are not well understood or possible, and the difference between psycho-education on a disorder and skills building needs to be clear.

In public health, specialising and dealing with a clientele all experiencing a similar difficulty means that CBT specialisation is possible. But specialising can make checks and balances and supervision more difficult. Who is eligible to provide technical supervision to a person who may be the only clinician who is an expert in a narrowly defined patient group?

Private practice on the other hand, requires a more generalised skill set and competence in many disorders, and challenges tend to be around work needing to be done away from face to face contact. A good example of this is exposure treatment. The essential component of an effective anxiety treatment is exposure. How effectively can exposure be done in a 50-minute session? How can an exposure session be planned and arranged? In a CAMHS (child and adolescent mental health service), I had time to either make phone calls, plan the session and source material needed; for example, a dog, dog poo, balloons, and so on.

## Future Directions

This chapter is a call for greater honesty around what kinds of CBT treatments are difficult/easy or being done/not being done in common treatment settings.

Key questions for any practitioner to ask themselves include (1) How easily/quickly can I get hold of evidence-based material to guide my practice?; (2) Does my treatment actually require other people or the creation of a virtual team (such as a GP in the community for an anorexic patient and regular appointments with medical personnel being set up and being adhered to by the patients)?; (3) Does the way I am practicing bear any resemblance to the evidence-based manu-

alised treatment for this disorder?; (4) Can the most efficacious of strategies be done or are they really too time
consuming to make work?; (5) Is the dropout rate of a certain
clientele higher or lower than what is put forward in the
research and what might be some of the reasons behind that?;
and (6) How much out of session work does this evidence-
based treatment require and how will it be done?

## Further Readings

Cronin, T.J., Lawrence, K.A, Taylor, K., Norton, P.J., & Kazantzis, N.
(2015). Integrating between-session interventions
(homework) in therapy: The importance of the therapeutic
relationship and cognitive case conceptualization. *Journal of
Clinical Psychology, 71*(5), 439–450.

Thwaites, R., Bennett-Levy, J., Davis, M., & Chaddock, A. (2014).
Using self-practice and self-reflection (SP/SR) to enhance CBT
competence and metacompetence. In A. Whittington, & N.
Grey (Eds). *How to become a more effective CBT therapist:
Mastering metacompetence in clinical practice.* (pp. 241–254).
London, England: Wiley-Blackwell.

Waller G. (2009). Evidence-based treatment and therapist drift.
*Behaviour Research and Therapy, 47,* 119–127.

0 1341 1717838 1

CPSIA information can be obtained
at www.ICGtesting.com
Printed in the USA
FFHW01n1334130818
47778614-51457FF

9 781922 117700